THEM/

MW01532191

The Practical Approach to Sermon Preparation

By Pastor David C. Green

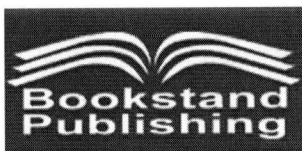

Bookstand
Publishing

www.bookstandpublishing.com

Published by
Bookstand Publishing
Morgan Hill, CA 95037
3893_5

ISBN 978-1-61863-522-8

Printed in the United States of America

Dedicated to the memory of Dr. Floyd Hays Barackman. Professor, mentor and friend. He encouraged me long ago to put my thoughts into writing. "The greatest theologian in New York State"(JLB).

FOREWORD

Have you been to church lately? I hope so. And if you have, you and I as church-goers have been part of the most biblically ignorant church since the first century. That sounds a bit harsh so let me say it another way. In the history of Christianity, our church congregations have never been bigger, they have never been richer, and they have never been less informed by God's Word.

Think about it. In your church, there is somebody who can tell you to the square inch the size of your auditorium. In your church, there is somebody who can tell you to the person how many people attended your services. In your church, there is somebody who can tell you to the penny how much the offering was last Sunday. But in your church, there is nobody who can tell you if or how much your congregation has grown in personal spiritual maturity in the previous week.

As a church we have run into the buzz-saw of Bible illiteracy. When I first spoke of this plague decades ago, no one was convinced. Today, no one needs to be convinced. We face a serious deficiency in our knowledge of the only book God ever wrote.

But there is an answer to this problem. In fact there are many of them. For one thing, people could read their Bibles. If people blew the dust off there Bibles at the same time, we'd all be killed in the dust storm. That's taking personal responsibility for our journey toward spiritual maturity. But there is also a group activity that will enhance our understanding of God and His plans for us. It is church, that same church where we count people, square feet and money. And there is one key element in church that has historically made a significant contribution both to enhancing spiritual growth and encouraging personal Bible engagement. It's preaching. Meaningful, substantive, biblical preaching.

Albert Mohler was right when he said, "Churches must recover the centrality and urgency of biblical teaching and preaching, and refuse to sideline the teaching ministry of the preacher. Pastors and churches too busy--or too distracted--to make biblical knowledge a central aim of ministry will produce believers who simply do not know enough to be faithful disciples."

But for preaching to be effective it requires three things: 1) it must be biblical, based in the Word of God; 2) it must be memorable, able for the mind to follow the preacher; and 3) it must be life-changing, making a difference to its hearers.

Often preaching that is biblical and even life-changing is not memorable because of a lack of organization, logic and movement to a conclusion. That's where the science of homiletics comes in. A sermon is like a body. You see the face, the eyes, the hair, the muscles and you are moved. You like what you see. But what you don't see, the skeleton, is what holds everything else in place and gives substance to the body. Unfortunately, sermon structure is often absent from much preaching today and thus the impact of the sermon is unnecessarily hampered.

Pastor David C. Green has been schooled in a logical approach to creating a sermon that aids in making the message memorable. But beyond that, he has been thoughtful in improving; explaining and advancing the homiletics he was taught. This book is the fruit of his thoughtfulness.

If as Pierre Ch. Marcel says. "Preaching is the central, primary function of the church," and it is, everyone who is called to handle the Word of God, whether preacher, Bible study leader, or Sunday school teacher, should be interested in making their message more memorable.

In the pages that follow you will find help both for your preparation and for your listeners' understanding when you present God's Word. That is a worthy goal for both of you.

Dr. Woodrow Kroll

Lincoln, Nebraska

TABLE OF CONTENTS

PREFACE

My first experience preaching was at a Spanish-speaking church in Ecuador, South America. I was only 21 at the time and was serving as a short-term missionary. Being the "new kid on the block" I knew that the leadership would eventually ask me to speak so I prepared myself for the bombshell that would blow my feelings of peace and safety to smithereens. Each time I thought of speaking to a crowd of people anxiety gripped my soul in spite of the vain attempts to suppress it. It was one of those occasions in life where you are at perfect peace as long as you are not thinking of something imminently dreadful. As soon as it comes to mind, of course, the fears erupt to the surface like a volcano and leave you as petrified as stone. Perhaps those leaders didn't give it a second thought but if they knew how insecure I felt they probably would have rescinded the offer. The weight of proclaiming God's Word was heavier on me than a ton of bricks. Not only was my self-confidence lacking but I had never learned to preach a sermon. I can honestly say that it was one of the loneliest times of my life.

"How would I do this?" was the question that terrorized my mind as I visualized myself panicking with stage fright the moment I opened my mouth. I did the only thing I knew to do. I picked up an audio tape of John MacArthur's sermon on I Corinthians 13, the love chapter, and preached that. I think his sermon is one of the best messages ever preached on the subject. I listened to it over and over and memorized it till I knew it inside and out. Essentially, I preached his sermon. Plagiarism at that point was not my concern- I did it out of ignorance. Nevertheless, because I put my heart into it that audiotaped message became my message and God used it to bless the people who heard it. Needless to say, this method of preaching, although permissible for a first-time novice, is not acceptable for someone who steps into the pulpit weekly.

The place where I was taught to preach was in my homiletics class at Davis College. My professor said that if you can preach in a homiletics class you can preach anywhere. He was right. Classmates are not the most sympathetic lot in the church. Nevertheless we were all introduced to the most logical and versatile system of homiletics ever devised (can you tell I am biased?). What we realized very early was that there is no one method that instructs the same way. It is not like the subject of English grammar whereby everyone agrees to the same set of rules. Each professor goes about the task using his own method in spite of the fact that there are certain things everyone would agree to. The differences, however, are enough to confuse a student as to which is right.

Does the subject of homiletics possess an intrinsic set of rules the way grammar governs English? If it does then to my knowledge there is no system that reflects it definitively. When a budding preacher is looking for help and can't find it perhaps the best thing to do is to study what everyone else has to say about the subject. He might be able to comprise a unique system that is both logical and useful. The value of what he creates will be determined by the many pastors and evangelists who use it regularly. A good place to start for such a preacher is to identify the similarities between the various methods of sermon preparation and go from there. One thing that any reputable institution would agree to: Every sermon must possess an identifiable theme. Regardless of the style or form of presentation there must be one central idea that governs the message. All aspects of the sermon must be developed around it and reflect it clearly. If not then the sermon will lack both purpose and coherence.

Theological institutions across the globe have made their contributions to the field of study and those contributions speak for themselves with the men who have preached the Gospel to millions. There have been tens of thousands of preachers who never had the privilege of studying in school but God has used them regardless. I want to make it clear that this author's intention is not to downgrade anyone who has developed their own system that works for them. God's Word will not return void. My intention for writing is simply to aid those faithful servants of God who could benefit from a few simple pointers given in this book. If there is an intrinsic set of rules for homiletics this author's quest is to do his best in identifying it. In my opinion the founders of Davis College have come as close as anyone. If I can fill in some gaps to what these men have already blessed us with then I have truly accomplished something significant. The reader will have to be the judge of that. This set of rules has been previously termed *The Practical Approach* which I have coined *Thematic Preaching* in order to emphasize its essential nature.

Pastor David C. Green
Living Faith Bible Church
         Sauquoit, NY

CHAPTER ONE

The Theme

THE CENTRALITY OF THE THEME

The preacher stepped to the podium as he opened his message with a resounding boom, "Are you ready to meet your maker!" He then related a heart-felt, personal experience of how one of his friends died young as they were playing football. It was touching, tear-jerking, and seemed to put the congregation in a serene and serious frame of mind. The impact it had on his life was obvious and the congregation knew it. The emotions it aroused subtly shifted the focus for the need to live your life to the fullest. Using the story of missionary C.T. Studd he passionately described this man's intensity as he fulfilled his work of service to the African people.

Naturally, this led him to discuss the importance of perseverance. He reiterated Sir Winston Churchill's famous quotation, *"Never give in, never give in, never; never; never; never - in nothing, great or small, large or petty - never give in except to convictions of honor and good sense,"* as he implored his congregation to bear up under hardships. As his message was winding down he added, *"Love is the only way you can accomplish this feat."* He closed his message with the Apostle Paul's declaration of true love found in 1st Corinthians 13 and elaborated on its deep meaning.

The people's heads were buzzing after his powerful presentation and their thoughts raced to and fro as they tried to make sense of it all. Their faces portrayed a question-mark as if they were all asking themselves the same thing at the same time: *"What was the purpose of this this sermon?"* His message, though passionate, did not possess one specific theme nor did it sufficiently drive home one particular lesson but instead it seemed like four mini sermons: Being ready to die, living life to the fullest, persevering through tough times, and having love.

Is this the only congregation that left church wondering what point the preacher was trying to make as a result of his sermon? Probably not. Every sermon should have a specific purpose. What does the preacher want the people to realize or to do as a result of his message? What is the core idea of that purpose? Whatever it is it must be stated in a succinct, specific manner that the audience can clearly understand. This succinct statement is called a theme. It describes the overall idea, purpose or central motif whether it concerns a biblical message, theatrical play, literary work, or any other genre.

Laurence Perrine, English literary scholar, states *"To derive the theme of a story, we must ask what its central purpose is: what view of life it supports or what insight into life it reveals."*[1] The theme, therefore, reveals the author's intentions for writing. It delineates the underlying moral (if there is one because, in fact, not all literary works have one) and sums up the gist of a story into a concise description. When a reader can state the theme he has proven that he has a grip on the heart and soul of what he is reading. Themes, therefore, have an important place in the subject of literature.

---

[1] Laurence Perrine, *Literature, Structure, Sound, and Sense*, 5th ed. (New York: Harcourt Brace Jovanovich Publishers, 1988), 90.

For example, the theme of Shakespeare's play *Othello* is *Jealousy Exacts a Terrible Cost.* In contrast, the theme of *Moby Dick* could be summarized as *Revenge is a Lethal, Self-Inflicting Poison.* Are these themes easily recognizable? Anyone who has knowledge of either of them would say yes. Likewise, a sermon's theme must be stated in the same kind of succinct and concise manner summing up the moral of the story. After hearing a sermon listeners should be able to state its theme as easily as they could summarize *Moby Dick's.*

Themes, therefore, have a "moral" element to them making them particularly important to the subject of homiletics. I think we all would agree that *Moby Dick's* theme teaches us a worthy lesson about the danger of unchecked revenge. Is that the reason why Herman Melville wrote it? Did he want to save the public from this terrible vice? Probably not. The story line makes it very entertaining to read and that, no doubt, is why he penned the masterpiece. My point, of course, is that if *Moby Dick's* theme teaches us a worthy lesson about life how much more should the theme of a biblical message?

In an organizational sense, themes of sermons stand in the limelight of both importance and practicality. They should stick out like sore thumbs and take center stage in the introduction, body, and the conclusion of a message. They are the heart and soul of what the preacher is saying and reveal the central motif and purpose to the audience. This book will demonstrate that all the subject matter of a sermon centers on the theme. And, if it is possible to deliver a good, coherent message that is not centered on the theme, the reader will not find it here.

The most important aspect of any sermon, therefore, is the theme. The entire contents of the sermon body must reflect it clearly. If it does not then the sermon will lack coherence and the listener will leave thinking the preacher was not sure about what he wanted to say. Even if the sermon has many inspiring points if the hearers cannot discern a clear theme they will not know the purpose of the message. They will hear different pieces of information and not know how they relate to one another. Sermons like this tend to be broad in nature but lack depth. A well stated theme, however, acts as glue which keeps the body of the sermon coherent, unified, and focused one main idea.

People do not come to church to be entertained (at least they shouldn't) or, for that matter, just to hear biblical information. They come to be spiritually motivated, challenged, and inspired personally. Messages people remember are ones that instill in their minds a specific lesson or point. They remember it because it had a "punch factor" that spoke to them personally. This is where a well stated theme comes into play. The theme sets the stage for a specific, concise lesson the preacher wants to convey to his audience. When themes in sermons are vague or too broad they often fail to deliver the desired impact that people remember for a long time to come.

Can a preacher deliver a wallop if his theme is vague? Undoubtedly, yes, but when he does it is because the truth of God's Word speaks loud and clear regardless of his ability to deliver coherent messages. Nevertheless, if it is possible with a vague theme how much more so in a sermon characterized by one central motif that builds to a crescendo and drives one specific lesson home? Much greater indeed! *The Sermon on the Mount*, the greatest sermon ever preached by anyone, has a concise theme which everything else relates to: *Heavenly Righteousness as Opposed to the Righteousness of the Scribes and Pharisees*. If you don't believe me, read it.

While the above principles are true and a novice would do very well in heeding them God uses people regardless of their inadequacies and inability to create organized sermons. The Spirit of God is the one who makes the final impact. This, perhaps, is the most important piece of advice given in this book: *Unless the Lord builds the house, they labor in vain that built it* (Ps. 127:1)[2]. More important than devising a good theme is the preacher's surrender to the Spirit of God and the willingness to listen to that still small voice. More important than narrowing a broad subject down to a good, central motif is the preacher's willingness to put down his own wisdom and strength in order to become "vulnerable" and "weak" under the power of the Holy Spirit. Delivering sermons is a spiritual task and, therefore, no matter of organization, high-powered delivery, or pithy wisdom will serve as substitutes for it. Rest assured, however, the Spirit of God honors those who work hard to deliver His Word effectively. When the Spirit of God delivers a message it always has purpose.

---

[2] All biblical references henceforth are in the KJV unless otherwise specified as the NKJV. *New King James Version* ®Copyright ©1982 by Thomas Nelson, Inc. Used by Permission. All Rights Reserved.

In general, the narrower a theme is the better. The reason is because it means that all the unnecessary verbiage is eliminated leaving only the nugget of truth. This truth is what makes the biblical passage relevant to the audience. Unfortunately, it's not always an easy to task to come up with a concise, specific theme because some scriptural texts do not warrant them. Their literary dynamics make it impossible.

For example, historical narrative tells us what happened but it does not necessarily try to teach a moral lesson as a result. It's hard to state a concise theme when there isn't one. Hence, the theme will consist of a generalized description of the subject matter rather than a phrase or sentence chock full of moral lessons. Its theme, therefore, may be vaguer than what is typically desired. The preacher is left to make the necessary applications and word his theme in a way that does justice to his sermon. He will restrict his theme in order to make it relevant to his congregation. The themes of historical narrative, therefore, are often more challenging when it comes to applying spiritual principles to everyday life.

An example of a sermon with a broader-than-usual theme is recorded in Acts 7 concerning Stephen, the first martyr. In defending himself, Stephen wanted to give the Sanhedrin a reality check in order to make it clear who the guilty party really was. A broad theme such as this one is useful in such cases particularly when the preacher is trying to give an overview of a topic. Stephen recited Israel's long and sinful history to an audience that was not thrilled about what he had to say. His theme, *Israel's Past History of Sin*, was very effective and accomplished his express intention of convicting them of their evil deeds. So effective, in fact, they murdered him for it. He delivered a lot of information to them but it certainly delivered the punch factor in spite of its breadth.

The fact that his message was effective does not negate the principle that the narrower a theme is the better. It only demonstrates that the preacher is using a weapon appropriate for the desired target. Rifles are used for land animals but shotguns are used for birds. Both have specific targets and both are lethal. One, however, is used for depth and the other breadth.

Let's look at the theme, *The Death of Christ*. Depending upon what the preacher intends on saying, it may be fine to preach in one sermon. On the other hand it may be too broad to do it justice. The preacher's approach when handling it will be the determining factor. A novice is more likely to pick a broad theme because he knows he can easily find a lot of information to talk about. He is not worrying about driving a point home, he is worrying about surviving. As he grows in experience and confidence a surface handling of important topics will not suffice him. He will then desire to narrow it in order to speak more thoroughly and deeply about it. For example, *The Kinds of Death Christ Died*. Or, *The Eternal Benefits of Christ's Death*. Or, *The Necessity of Christ's Death*. All of these are narrow aspects of the overall subject of Christ's Death.

Let's look at another example: *Praising God*. We can narrow it to *The Biblical Command to Praise God*. Or, *The Importance of Praising God*. Or, *The Spiritual Benefits of Praising God*, etc. You can see that the broad theme, *Praising God*, is narrowed to one specific aspect of it. This allows the speaker to go much deeper with his presentation. The preacher could, in fact, keep the same broad theme and use the narrowed aspects as his major points. The result, however, will be a general overview on the subject, which is fine, depending on what he intends on accomplishing.

Let's use one more example, *Obedience*. Too vast to handle in one sermon we could constrict it this way: *The Difficulty of Obedience*. Or, *The Importance of Obedience*. Or, *The Spiritual Benefits of Obedience,* etc. In each case the broader subject is narrowed to one aspect of it. This tells the listener that the preacher has something specific to teach about obedience.

The paradoxical factor about narrowing a theme is that while it should be concise (meaning as few words as possible) it should also be specific (requiring more words to describe it). On the one hand you must eliminate all unnecessary terms to keep it short but on the other you must describe it more specifically. The by-product of this mental exercise, however, is a power-packed description that your congregation will fully grasp and easily follow as you progress through your sermon.

THE FIVE RULES FOR A GOOD THEME

We stated sufficiently that a good theme is a narrow one but for repetition's sake our first rule of thumb is **Brevity**. Typically, the shorter and more narrow the theme the better it is as long as you are adequately describing the main thrust of what you want to say.

Second, **Consistency**. The theme you choose must remain the central idea and driving force in each and every main point of your sermon body. If it does not then you have chosen a wrong theme or have gone off on a tangent.

Third, **Flexibility**. Herein lays the beauty of *Thematic Preaching*. If a speaker chooses a theme but it is not accomplishing what he intends and it is not taking him where he wants to go then he has chosen a wrong theme. He has the freedom and flexibility to change it providing he is being faithful to the text. He should never feel constricted as if he is being disobedient. The Lord allows that freedom because that is the way He leads His people in delivering His Word. This takes into account, of course, that the preacher is being sensitive to the direction of the Spirit.

Fourth, **Simplicity**. As a rule the more simple a theme is the easier it is to preach and the easier it is for the listeners to understand. Naturally, there are exceptions to this rule but it helps if he can state his central motif with simplicity. Lengthiness, awkward language, and extended themes complicate things. Simplicity, however, does not mean being broad. Simple themes are often very specific.

In this same vein compound themes should be avoided because by their very nature they introduce more than one central idea. Here is an example: *The Prayers and Tribulations of Paul*. What are you preaching, the prayers of Paul or the tribulations of Paul? What we have here are two individual themes that are not related at all. How can the preacher do justice to both in one sermon? The exception to this rule would be compound themes that state the same thing. For example: *The Trials and Tribulations of Paul*. Trials and tribulations are only synonyms and, therefore, are not in conflict with each other. Actually, this theme is not really compound with respect to subject matter but only in the sense of sentence structure. The compound form is poetic in nature.

Fifth, **phraseology.** That is, state your theme as a phrase and not as a complete sentence. Generally themes are stated as complete sentences or even paragraphs (for books etc.) but for sermons it is best to state the theme as a phrase. The reason is because sentences are complete statements in and of themselves containing both subject and predicate. There is nothing more to say about them.

Let's use an example of a theme taken from I Kings 19:4 (see below). Elijah felt like he was on the brink of dying because he was so overwhelmed. *The Spiritual Dangers of Over-Exhaustion* will serve as a good theme for that passage. What if we stated that phrase as a complete sentence instead? *Over-exhaustion will cause spiritual dangers such as depression and discouragement, etc.* This complete statement does not lend itself to being developed further. You a have stated what you had to say and now the people can go home. A theme stated as a phrase, however, lends itself to further inquiry. A sentence does not.

THE DIFFERENCE BETWEEN A THEME AND A TITLE

What is the difference between a title and a theme? After all, they seem to be similar in ways. In some ways they are but they are different in others because they serve a different purpose. A theme is the central idea of the sermon. All the subject matter of the sermon body reflects it clearly. A title, on the other hand, is just a catchy phrase that is intended to whet the audience's appetite for what is to follow. Like themes titles inform the listener as to the

13

gist of the sermon. Titles, however, do not lend themselves to being developed into main points. That is not their purpose. Titles are poetic in nature and serve as an aid both to the preacher and to the audience. They benefit the preacher because they help him keep to his theme and they benefit the audience by letting them know where the preacher is going.

Let's look at I Kings 19:4 in the Old Testament and find both the theme and title.

But he (Elijah) went a day's journey into the wilderness, and came and sat down under a juniper tree: and he requested for himself that he might die; and said, It is enough; now, O LORD, take away my life; for I am not better than my fathers.

The sermon theme for this verse could be *The Spiritual Danger of Over-Exhaustion.* Elijah wanted to die because of his wearisome battles with Ahab and Jezebel but the Lord caused him to rest and told him that he could not fight in his own strength. The main idea of this verse is that over-extending ourselves without God's help can cause spiritual and physical fatigue followed by depression and discouragement. This is the gist of the sermon and can be completely developed as the sermon progresses. The title, on the other hand, could be *Has the Zip Gone out of your Zap?* This catchy phrase explains what the sermon is about and arouses the audience's desire to hear it. That is what a good title does.

Here's another example of the difference between a theme and a title. *The Story of the Prodigal Son* is the theme of Luke 15 but the title could be *Blood is Thicker than Mud* or *The Hog Pen Trail.* Both of these titles were taken from actual sermons of preachers and poetically relate the gist of the sermon while inciting the audience's curiosity as to what will follow.[3]

At this point it is a good idea to learn how to choose a theme. This subject invariably leads us to understand the difference between topical, textual, and expository sermons. The reason is because in each of these the preacher must derive his theme accordingly. I will briefly define these sermon types now but will handle them in much more detail later.

CHOOSING A THEME FOR THE TOPICAL SERMON

A topical sermon is one wherein the preacher creates a theme from his own ideas about something and does not necessarily rely upon a specific scriptural text in order to get it. This does not imply that it is unbiblical. It only means that the preacher is not using a particular passage to do so. Using that theme he may use different, relevant verses in order to create his main points. For example, *Why God's Love is So Vast* is an easy theme to develop. This subject came from an idea I already had about God's love and I didn't extract it from any one passage of Scripture. Choosing a theme, therefore, in topical sermons comes from meditating on God's Word and how it affects our lives. The sermon body might look like this:

Example:

---

[3] *Blood is Thicker than Mud,* a sermon written and preached by Pastor Hiawatha Hemphill of the Servant's Heart Worship Center, High Point, NC. *The Hog Pen Trail*, preached by the late Pastor E.V. Hill, Mt. Zion Missionary Baptist Church in Los Angeles, at spiritual emphasis week at Liberty University.

Theme: *Why God's Love is So Vast*
Main Points:

    I.   God's love is vast b/c it is secure (Rom. 8:38-39)
    II.   God's love is vast b/c it is gracious (I Pet. 2:3)
    III.   God's love is vast b/c it is jealous (Ex. 20:5-6)

CHOOSING A THEME FOR A TEXTUAL SERMON

By definition, a textual sermon is one where the preacher gets both his theme and main points directly from one (two or three at most) verse(s) of Scripture. Let's use an easy example in order to keep things simple.

Example: Micah 6:8

He hath shewed thee, O man, what is good; and what doth the LORD require of thee, but to do justly, and to love mercy, and to walk humbly with thy God?

Micah 6:8 makes easy work out of finding the theme and choosing main points. Let's take a look at it.

Theme: *What the Lord Requires of Us*
Main Points:

    I.   The Lord Requires us to do Justly
    II. The Lord Requires us to Love Mercy
    III. The Lord Requires us to Walk Humbly with Him

The simplicity of extracting both the theme and main points could not be easier using Micah 6:8. In the topical sermon plan the theme comes from the preacher's own ideas about the subject. The body of the sermon comes either from different passages of Scripture, the preacher's own life experience and knowledge on the subject, or one of our sermon approaches (see next chapter). In the textual sermon plan, however, the theme was already contained in the verse. The preacher did not have to go anywhere else to get it. The strength, therefore, of textual and expository sermons is that because their themes and main points are taken directly from the context of Scripture they are considered more authoritative.

CHOOSING A THEME FOR AN EXPOSITORY SERMON

By definition an expository sermon is one where the preacher gets the theme, main points, and any subpoints from more than two or more verses of the same passage of Scripture.

Example: Rev. 2:1-7

1Unto the angel of the church of Ephesus write; These things saith he that holdeth the seven stars in his right hand, who walketh in the midst of the seven golden candlesticks; 2I know thy works, and thy labour, and thy patience, and how thou canst not bear them which are evil: and thou hast tried them which say they are apostles, and are not, and hast found them liars: 3And hast borne, and hast patience, and for my name's sake hast laboured, and hast not fainted. 4Nevertheless I have somewhat against thee, because thou hast left thy first love. 5Remember therefore from whence thou art fallen, and repent, and do the first works; or else I will come unto thee quickly, and will remove thy candlestick out of his place, except thou repent. 6But this thou hast, that thou hatest the deeds of the Nicolaitans, which I also hate. 7He that hath an ear, let him hear what the Spirit saith unto the churches; To him that overcometh will I give to eat of the tree of life, which is in the midst of the paradise of God.

Theme: *The Message to the Church of Ephesus.*
Main Points:

     I.   The Leader of the Church (1)
     II. The Commendation to the Church (2,3,6)
     III. The Correction of the Church (4)
     IV. The Warning to the Church (5)

V.   The Admonition to the Church (7)

The main idea of the passage is that the Lord is giving a personal message to the church at Ephesus. That is the theme. The main points can easily be found by noticing the gist of each thing the Lord has to say to the church. In verse 1 the passage describes the One who is giving the message. That is, Christ, the head. In verse 2, 3, and 6 the Lord is commending the Ephesians for their hard work and commitment to purity. In verse 4 Christ informs the church that she has a major problem. Verse 5 warns her that if she doesn't correct the problem he will severely discipline her. Verse 7 concludes with a general admonition contained in all the messages to the seven churches to obey what is being spoken to them.

If we choose to alliterate the sermon for poetry's sake we may have something like this:

Theme: *The Message to the Church of Ephesus*
Main Points:

      I.   The Captain of the Church (1)
      II.   The Commendation to the Church (2,3,6)
      III.   The Correction of the Church (4)
      IV.   The Caution to the Church (5)
      V.   The Counsel to the Church (7)

This is not the time to go further in developing expository messages because I will handle it in great detail later. When we come to that point we will continue to practice choosing good themes as we look at various passages of Scripture. The important thing is that from the passage of Rev. 2:1-7 we have successfully extracted the theme and developed the entire sermon around it.

PRACTICE FINDING THE RIGHT THEME

Let's take a look at various passages of Scripture as well as other paragraphs of secular literature in order to practice finding the right theme for each one. Because the themes for topical sermons do not necessarily come from any one passage of Scripture it is not necessary to include them here. Textual and expository sermons, however, depend on the preacher's ability to correctly surmise the theme of the passage at hand. I cannot overstate the importance of this task. If a preacher cannot accurately state the theme of his sermon text he cannot intelligently represent that biblical truth in his sermon. The extent to which he uses a faulty theme is the same extent to which his sermon will lack authority. While finding the right theme is imperative, there is a proverb about the interpretation of Scripture: Scripture has only one interpretation but many applications. I think this statement has a lot of merit to it. Depending upon the genre there is a degree of flexibility in choosing a proper theme. The reason is because more than one application is possible concerning a particular text.

Example: 2 Samuel 9:1-13

Please look up and read the passage and then refer back to the discussion of its theme below.

I preached this message to my congregation a few months before writing this book. This historical passage depicts David's concern and care for the remaining relatives of King Saul. Saul was dead and David was established as king in his place. Because of his close relationship with Jonathan, Saul's son, David was determined to deal kindly with any living relatives of the deceased king. As fate would have it, Jonathan's son, Mephibosheth, was still alive. It was to him that David demonstrated that kindness.

There are two ways to portray this theme. First, we could state the theme as the historical fact - *David's Kindness to Mephibosheth* - giving the obvious idea of the text. I frequently use this approach when I am dealing with historical passages because it permits me to break the verses up easily into their component parts. Spiritual applications can then be drawn from those parts so that the passage becomes relevant to the lives of the audience. David's kindness to a member of an enemy house is the motif. What good would this be to us if we don't make any spiritual applications? The sermon must have more meaning for us today than the fact that David showed mercy to Mephibosheth. While the theme of David's kindness, therefore, is accurate it is also pointless without application.

If you use the historical-fact approach your sermon must somehow take a practical route in order to drive specific spiritual lessons home. When I use this method I often use a subtheme or title that points the listeners to the spiritual applications I want to make. For example, *David's Kindness to Mephibosheth: Dealing Graciously with the Undeserving*. The title/subtheme lays emphasis on the spiritual direction of the sermon while the principle theme makes it easy to divide the passage into its component parts for further development.

In contrast to the method above we can also state the theme more directly as follows: *The Bestowal of God's Grace*. The first instance stated the historical fact: David showed kindness to Mephibosheth. The second, however, cut through the chaff and went right to the spiritual lesson. In each case, however, we must apply spiritual principles to this historical passage even though we are handling it differently. The spiritual application is evident. Mephibosheth is like us. He is undeserving and helpless. This passage is a picture of Christ's unconditional mercy towards sinful humanity. We state the theme, therefore, as *The Bestowal of God's Grace*. When I preached this sermon I opted for the second method but typically I prefer the first. The context will dictate how you should handle each passage but in either case the motif, God's unmerited favor, should be presented as primary.

Example: Colossians 1:15-20

15 Who is the image of the invisible God, the firstborn of every creature: 16 For by him were all things created, that are in heaven, and that are in earth, visible and invisible, whether they be thrones, or dominions, or principalities, or powers: all things were created by him, and for him: 17 And he is before all things, and by him all things consist. 18 And he is the head of the body, the church: who is the beginning, the firstborn from the dead; that in all things he might have the preeminence. 19 For it pleased the Father that in him should all fulness dwell; 20 And, having made peace through the blood of his cross, by him to reconcile all things unto himself; by him, I say, whether they be things in earth, or things in heaven.

The Supremacy of Christ is the obvious theme of this passage. Everything in this text relates to Christ's superiority over anything else. All major divisions in the sermon body must be directly related to this motif. If they are not then the preacher has erred and gone off on a tangent.

Example: I Thessalonians 4:3-8

3 For this is the will of God, even your sanctification, that ye should abstain from fornication: 4 That every one of you should know how to possess his vessel in sanctification and honour; 5 Not in the lust of concupiscence, even as the Gentiles which know not God: 6 That no man go beyond and defraud his brother in any matter: because that the Lord is the avenger of all such, as we also have forewarned you and testified. 7 For God hath not called us unto uncleanness, but unto holiness. 8 He therefore that despiseth, despiseth not man, but God, who hath also given unto us his holy Spirit.

The Purity of the Believer would be the obvious choice here. Such examples make it easy to recognize the theme. Later, when we discuss expository preaching, we will learn how to derive main divisions from the theme.

Example: Hebrews 9:11-14

11 But Christ being come an high priest of good things to come, by a greater and more perfect tabernacle, not made with hands, that is to say, not of this building; 12 Neither by the blood of goats and calves, but by his own blood he entered in once into the holy place, having obtained eternal redemption for us. 13 For if the blood of bulls and of goats, and the ashes of an heifer sprinkling the unclean, sanctifieth to the purifying of the flesh: 14 How much more shall the blood of Christ, who through the eternal Spirit offered himself without spot to God, purge your conscience from dead works to serve the living God?

The theme for this Scripture is *The Superiority of the Blood of Christ.* Not all passages that you decide to preach yield their themes this easily. I have used these examples only to demonstrate the fact that in every case you are looking for a central idea. You must identify the overall motif if your sermon is going to accurately portray the intentions of the biblical writers.

Example: Psalm 1:1-6

Blessed is the man that walketh not in the counsel of the ungodly, nor standeth in the way of sinners, nor sitteth in the seat of the scornful. 2

But his delight is in the law of the Lord; and in his law doth he meditate day and night. 3 And he shall be like a tree planted by the rivers of water, that bringeth forth his fruit in his season; his leaf also shall not wither; and whatsoever he doeth shall prosper. 4 The ungodly are not so: but are like the chaff which the wind driveth away. 5 Therefore the ungodly shall not stand in the judgment, nor sinners in the congregation of the righteous. 6 For the Lord knoweth the way of the righteous: but the way of the ungodly shall perish.

The motif of Psalm 1 is that there are two ways, two destinies, two choices that every person is faced with: The way of godliness versus the way of wickedness. We will state the theme, therefore, as *A Contrast Between the Way of the Wicked To the Way of the Godly.* The entire passage expresses that truth. Not all Psalms, however, are that easy to describe. Many of them are long with free-flowing thoughts that shift between devotional sentiments and repetitive statements. The Book of Psalms is perhaps the most difficult genre of literature when it comes to outlining homiletical structure. They are written in a poetic fashion and their themes and major points are difficult to pinpoint and trace.

Example: Coach Les Steckel's book, <u>One Yard Short</u>.

As I got to know more about Preppie and her background, I found myself powerfully drawn to her family. She was and is one of those products of a truly loving household. I've always had reverence for both my parents and the home I came from, and I've always been grateful for the life lessons I learned there. But there were some special dynamics in Chris Pickett's family that I knew I craved.[4]

What is the theme of this paragraph? How about *Chris Pickett's Loving Household*? That is the gist of this short

---

[4] Coach Les Steckel, <u>One Yard Short</u> (Nashville: Thomas Nelson Publishers, 2006), 48.

paragraph. If the only portion of <u>One Yard Short</u> that someone read was this paragraph he could tell you, if nothing else, that the author admired Chris Pickett's loving home and family. If I wanted to develop a sermon around this theme I would find as many aspects of the loving household that I could find in the paragraph and make main divisions from them. If I stated the theme as, *The Author's Disappointment with His Own Home Life Compared to Chris Pickett's*, I would be misrepresenting the gist of this paragraph. The author was not disappointed with his own home life. He stated that clearly. He simply said that there was something about Chris Pickett's home that he craved. There was a dynamic that his friend's home had that his didn't. This is quite different from being disappointed with his own home life. If you make this kind of mistake with a sermon text you will be misrepresenting the Bible to the congregation.

Example: David Dolan's book, <u>Holy War for the Promised Land</u>

In May 1921, widespread Arab violence broke out against the growing Jewish community. Armed Arab bands attacked Haifa, Petach Tikva, Jaffa, and two other towns. The Jaffa riots were the bloodiest - forty seven Jews lost their lives. Zionist leaders still publicly speaking about their hopes of amicable Jewish/Arab relations, were beginning to realize that local Arabs were determined to do everything in their power to prevent the establishment of a Jewish state. They feared that British authorities would cave in to the growing Arab violence and go back on their pledge to set up a Jewish homeland.[5]

The theme for this paragraph could be stated as follows: *The Fears of the Zionist Leaders that the Creation of a*

---

[5]David Dolan, <u>Holy War for the Promised Land</u> (Nashville: Thomas Nelson Publishers, 1991), 81.

Jewish State Would Never Come to Pass Amid Violent Arab Opposition. This is the gist of this paragraph. Zionist leaders feared that Israel would never come into existence because of the bloody Arab-led riots. If we wanted to shorten the theme further we could say, *The Zionist Leaders Fear for their Desired Homeland.* In either case the key words are *Zionist Leaders, Fear,* and *Homeland.* These key words express the main idea of the paragraph. Let's look at a few examples in order to find the right theme for the textual method of sermon preparation.

Example: Isaiah 40:31

31 But they that wait upon the Lord shall renew their strength; they shall mount up with wings as eagles; they shall run, and not be weary; and they shall walk, and not faint.

Our choice for this theme would be *The Blessedness of Waiting Upon the Lord,* or curtailed a bit, *Waiting Upon the Lord.* It is the gist and main idea of the verse. Everything in the sermon body should reflect this idea closely.

Example: John 3:18

He that believeth on him is not condemned: but he that believeth not is condemned already, because he hath not believed in the name of the only begotten Son of God.

The Absolute Necessity of Believing in Jesus is the only possible theme for this verse. It is possible to alter it a little but the main idea is that without believing in Jesus a person is lost. There is not much wiggle room in this passage.

Example: Ephesians 2:3

Among whom also we all had our conversation in times past in the lusts of our flesh, fulfilling the desires of the flesh and of the mind; and were by nature the children of wrath, even as others.

Our Former Lost Condition is a logical choice. The verse depicts our former lives that were filled with our evil, fleshly desires and we were considered by God to be by nature children of wrath.

Example: Psalm 63:1

O God, thou art my God; early will I seek thee: my soul thirsteth for thee, my flesh longeth for thee in a dry and thirsty land, where no water is;

The Psalmist's Cry for the Presence of the Lord is a good theme for this verse. You could substitute the pronoun "our" or the phrase "the believer's" in place of *psalmist* in order to personalize it but the idea remains the same. When God is absent the believer yearns for His presence just as the body craves for water when parched.

These few examples of finding the right themes are just a taste of more to come as we delve into the expository method of preaching. They are intended to expose you to the importance of finding the right theme of your sermon text.

CHAPTER TWO

The Topical Sermon

A Topical sermon is one in which a preacher chooses a theme from his own general understanding of a topic and then uses other Scriptures, etc. in order to create the main points of his sermon body. For example, *Relying on God's Strength* may be a sermon theme that I decide to preach. Perhaps I have been thinking about this idea for a long time. I might even use a key verse when I introduce that message. I may open the sermon with Ephesians 6:10, *Finally, my brethren, be strong in the Lord, and in the power of his might.* Unless I get my main points from that same verse, however, it is still considered a topical message because the main points are taken either from other Scriptures or somewhere else.

Topical does not imply that it is not biblical. It only means that the preacher is not getting his theme and main points from the same passage(s) of Scripture. Textual and Expository sermons, however, get both their themes and main points from a single passage. Admittedly, you may get your theme from another passage of Scripture as in the above topical example but by definition a topical message does not depend upon this.

Earlier I used *The Vastness of God's Love* as an example of a theme for a topical sermon plan. Although this looks simple to create it is easy to become confused and make mistakes. Those mistakes will in turn confuse the audience. An aspiring preacher should take great care making sure he follows the rules of thumb given earlier regarding the selection and use of a theme.

Topical sermon plans are the easiest to construct. They tend to be a little better to use for sermons on special occasions. Textual and expository messages restrict you to the text at hand. Their strength is also their weakness. Rest assured, being restricted to a biblical text is not a weakness under the right conditions. It gives a sense of unprecedented biblical authority. Topical messages, however, allow a great amount of freedom which may be necessary when you are speaking about something unique. You may not find one passage of Scripture that will do your theme justice. You may have to jump around in the Bible in order to drive it home. Remember, topical does not mean unbiblical. Many great preachers used nothing but topical messages. Evangelists and revivalists tend to be topical preachers.

Whether textual, expository, or topical, however, good homiletics stresses the consistency and effectiveness of using and tracing the theme. There are many great preachers who never used the expository method but I can assure you that their sermons contain concise themes which they adequately emphasized in their messages. You will see examples of famous messages from all three sermon types later in this book.

At this point in time the question at hand is, "now that I know what a topical sermon is how do I create the main points?" The difficulty with any of the sermon types is devising main points once you have decided upon a theme. If you don't know what you are doing you may get lucky and preach a sermon that is coherent. When you have to do it every Sunday, however, you will find out how difficult the task really is. Bad habits are formed in the early days of a preacher's career. We want to start out on the right foot.

Perhaps in the past your pastor asked you to preach once. You knew exactly what you wanted to say because God had given you a message through great and trying circumstances in your life. Your message had been stirring in your heart for a long time. When you wrote out your sermon plan your main points naturally coincided with your theme and your sermon was very coherent. It had the "punch factor" to it. The reason it was coherent was because you had a concise theme and knew exactly what to say about it. That's great! Now do it every week and have the same effect. A novice will get "lucky" once in a while but preaching every week requires some help. We need some pattern or device that will help us derive main points once we have a good theme in mind.

The late Dr. Gordon C. Davis, president of Davis College (1934—1961, Johnson City, NY), evidently realized that unless his students had some help they would continually struggle writing topical sermons. He is credited for developing a unique system of homiletics (which I have coined *Thematic Preaching*) that develops a sermon around its theme. While other systems of homiletics may claim to do the same thing Dr. Davis's method is by far the most complete and systematic. His method is known as *The Practical Approach* (Davis College was formerly called Practical Bible Training School). Whether preaching topically, textually, or expositorily, his focus was that each and every point of the sermon body must reflect the theme clearly. In order to accomplish this he came up with a way of mechanically extracting main points from the theme in topical sermons. Obviously, if the main points come directly from the theme the sermons would be coherent and have purpose. He called his method of devising main points *devices* and/or *approaches.*

The late Dr. John Benson, my professor of homiletics at Davis College, refined the system significantly. In addition, Dr. Woodrow Kroll, current radio talk show host of *Back To The Bible,* alumnus, and former president of Davis College (1981- 1990), also contributed greatly to this system that is recorded in his book <u>The Prescription for Preaching</u>.[6] The approaches I am about to show you, therefore, come primarily from the hard work of these three men. Many others have contributed in their own way by preserving its practicality in their sermon preparation. Dr. Benson states the usefulness of these mechanical devices this way:

I want to give you some devices which will divide the theme mechanically. These devices and mechanical aids will enable you to draw from the theme far more than you possibly ever imagine is in it. I call these devices which are applied to the theme APPROACHES. By APPROACH I mean the way in which we go about handling or developing the theme into its component parts.[7]

A Disclaimer About Using These Approaches

The approaches I am about to show you serve two purposes. First, they will arm you with practical tools that you can always fall back on should you run out of ideas when you are creating topical messages. Second, they will train your brain to think in a logical, parallel fashion that is

---

[6]Woodrow Michael Kroll, <u>The Prescription for Preaching</u> (Grand Rapids: Baker Book House, 1980).

[7] John L. Benson, <u>A System of Homiletics</u> 3rd ed. (Bible School Park, NY: by the author, 1986), 4.

absolutely essential to *Thematic Preaching*. It is not possible to jump into the biblical exposition that is taught in this book without learning these approaches first. Your brain needs to be trained first.

In addition, in teaching you these approaches I make no claim that they are the only means of creating good, topical messages. These approaches are intended to be the starting point of your preaching career, not the end. If you discipline yourself to learning them, however, you will set the stage for right thinking. They are training wheels of your sermon preparation skills as well as a logical format to follow should the need arise. Eventually you will make your own way and these approaches are there to help you get to that point.

THE "CHARACTERISTICS OF" APPROACH

The first mechanical device we will examine is called the "characteristics of" approach. By "characteristics of" we mean that we are going to take the key word of the theme and expound its characteristics. The key word will be a noun and therefore its modifier must be an adjective. Guardedly, participles and other verbals may also be used as long as their function is adjectival. Dr. Kroll states,

This approach to the topical sermon is designed to indicate the properties, marks, features, qualities, or characteristics of the theme. In essence, this is a descriptive approach. It describes the theme by indicating what the characteristics of the theme are.[8]

Here are several examples using the *"characteristics of" approach* along with the entire sermon plan.

Example:

---

[8] Kroll, 189.

Subject	Stewardship
Theme	A Good Steward of the Lord
Sermon Type	Topical
Approach	Characteristics Of
Purpose	To help Christians recognize a good steward of the Lord for who he is

Main Divisions:

I. One Characteristic of *a good steward of the Lord* is that he is faithful
II. Another characteristic of *a good steward of the Lord* is that he is loyal
III. A third characteristic of *a good steward of the Lord* is that he is honest

We used adjectives in each of the main points to modify *a good steward*. Good stewards are faithful, loyal and honest. That is the simplicity of this mechanical approach. In a sense we are extracting these main points from the theme by using the adjectives to describe the key noun. We are expressing the qualities of the key word of the theme. In order to do this we must use adjectives or at least something adjectival.

The Sermon Plan

The sermon plan in the previous example should not throw you for a loop. The items in it are obvious. We have already discussed the difference between a **subject** and a **theme**. We are currently using the **topical** method of preaching and we are using the "characteristics of" **approach** to do so. The only thing we haven't seen is the **purpose.** This, too, is obvious. Because we are expressing the characteristics, qualities, or nature of a good steward of the Lord we are helping you to see or to recognize what a good steward of the Lord is. It is to help the listener understand the nature of a thing. This sermon plan formula will essentially remain the same no matter what approach you are using.

Keep in mind that the specifics of the sermon plan should be reserved for the pastor's study. *Never bring these details (with this approach or any other) into the pulpit.* They are for your benefit to help you organize your thoughts. The only things you want to bring to the people are your theme, title (if you use one), and your main divisions. Any other information about the sermon plan is irrelevant to the audience.

Almost every book on homiletics contains the term **proposition** or **propositional statement**. I have taken the bold step and removed this phrase from the sermon plan because to me it is more confusing than it is helpful. In fact, homileticians often use it differently. As the meaning of the word implies it typically proposes to the congregation what the preacher intends on accomplishing. Because of its inconsistent use and because it is almost synonymous with the **purpose** I decided it would be easier to drop altogether. The full statement of your theme (as well as your subtheme and/or title) is more than sufficient to clue the audience in regard to what you want to accomplish.

To give you a bird's eye view of the "characteristics of" approach let me express the qualities of a few things just so you can realize its simplicity.

- *Boy Scouts of America* are trustworthy, loyal, helpful, friendly, courteous, kind, etc.

- *Reading the Bible* is insightful, mandatory, and beneficial.
- *The Resurrection of Christ* is supernatural, advantageous, and glorious.
- *The Destruction of the Wicked* is scriptural, sad, and imminent.
- *A True Friend* is consistent, dependable, and gracious.

As stated earlier, beginners should **write out the entire sermon plan** when preparing the message. Do not cut corners at this stage in the game. Our biggest enemy is getting ahead of ourselves and thinking that our own genius will get us through. One embarrassing sermon will cure you of that. Take the time and write out each thing in the sermon plan including the subject, theme, sermon type, approach, and purpose. This will keep you on track. The last point, the purpose, is what you intend on accomplishing as a result of the sermon. Because you are using the "characteristics of" approach you are describing the essential qualities of a good steward. Hence, as a result of your sermon people will be able to recognize what a good steward of the Lord is.

Rules of Thumb for "Characteristics Of"

1. Although it may seem tedious **write out "one characteristic," etc**. in every main division. As time progresses you can relax and drop the formalities but it is not wise to do so now. Discipline and consistency are the mediums that create good habits.
2. **Repeat the theme** just as you must repeat "one characteristic" in every main point. I cannot

overstate this. The reason is because it ensures that your main points are directly related to the theme. There is no chance of wandering. If you get lazy and drop it you will invariably lose track of it and go off on tangents. Your sermon will lose its coherence and purpose. Worse yet you will soon forget about relying on these mechanical devices and assume you can do better. You have just set the stage for limited sermon preparation ability and bad habits.

3. Be sure to *use a form of the state of being verb, to be* (i.e. is, are, am, was, were). Any other verb will not suffice. You are telling people the qualities of something. You are describing its nature. To do so you must use the state of being verb along with the predicate adjective. For example, the tree is tall. The boy is skinny. The road is wide. If you get careless and fail to follow the rules exactly you will begin by describing the qualities of something and then you will jump to what the thing does or has. When this happens the main points of your sermon will no longer be parallel. You told your audience what you intended to accomplish and then you switched to do something else.

4. *Do not use any other verbs with the state of being verb, to be*. For example, *The bird **is used** for making pillows.* The "characteristics of" approach means you are describing the traits or qualities of the bird. You are not telling what the bird is used for. The closest thing you could say is *the bird is useful.*

5. Following the finite verb, to be, **you must conclude with an adjective** (called the predicate adjective). You may use a verbal adjective or participle occasionally but be careful to retain parallel thoughts. For example, *the bird is* **large**. *The bird is* **tall**. If you then say *The bird is singing* you have followed the rules according to format but not function. You are not saying the same thing about the bird. You began by saying what the bird is (tall and large) and then said what the bird was doing. Context will dictate whether or not your thoughts remain parallel. You can get away with some things but if you push it the audience will detect your discontinuity.

6. Realize that both **your main divisions and theme may come from your own thoughts about a subject without directly relying on a particular biblical passage**. I stress this only to differentiate between creating themes and main points in topical sermons as opposed to textual and/or expository. In our example above, *A Good Steward of the Lord*, you might come up with the three characteristics on your own. There is nothing wrong with that. You may have had this on your mind for a long time. If it is true then certainly you will be able to back it up with Scripture. Obviously, if you don't back up your points with Scripture then your sermon is not authoritative. Your messages must always have their ultimate source in the truth of God's Word.

7. **Be sure your adjectives modify the right noun.** In other words, regarding the theme *A Good Steward*

of the Lord are you describing *a good steward* or are you describing the *Lord*? The subject of the sermon plan is stewardship, not Lord. Your main noun, therefore, is *steward* and your adjectives should only modify this.

Perhaps you think that I am going overboard and that it doesn't matter how parallel the main points should be. When you are talking about birds it may not matter but when you are talking about spiritual truth, life and death reality, communicating the message matters a lot. Parallelism will help to accomplish that.

Example:

Subject	Discipleship
Theme	A Disciple of the Lord
Type	Topical
Approach	Characteristics Of
Purpose	To help people understand what a disciple of the Lord is

Main Divisions:

    I. One characteristic of *a disciple of the Lord* is that he is patient

    II. Another characteristic of *a disciple of the Lord* is that he is persistent

    III. A third characteristic of *a disciple of the Lord* is that he is prayerful

Notice that I followed all the rules. I copied the entire sermon plan. I repeated the use of *one characteristic of* for each main division. I repeated the theme in each main point. I used the state of being verb, to be. I used only adjectives following the finite verb when describing the qualities of *a disciple of the Lord*. I did not add another verbal in order to modify the state of being verb, to be. Finally, I modified the right noun in the theme, *disciple*. Beginners will benefit greatly if they adhere steadfastly to these basic rules. We all wonder what we would preach if given that opportunity. Shouldn't we take advantage of the simplicity and ease of these mechanical approaches?

What if we wanted to say *A Disciple of the Lord* is surrendered, would that be permissible? Surrender is a verb but when put in the past tense it becomes adjectival. Yes, you can use it. For example, *a disciple of the Lord* is surrendered, saved, and satisfied. If you are going to use it then try to use it for your other main points as well. This is what we mean by maintaining parallelism. You will not always be able to do this. Following the rules keeps you on track with your theme but they are not intended to strait-jacket you. Sometimes you will not be able to be perfectly parallel but the audience will know exactly what you are saying anyway.

As a side note, in each of these themes the main noun that you are describing is the first one in every case. For example, the main noun in *The Word of God* is *Word*. You should be describing that, not God.

Example:

Subject	The Word
Theme	The Word of God
Type	Topical
Approach	Characteristics Of
Purpose	To help people recognize the Word of God for what it is

Main Divisions:

I. One characteristic of *the Word of God* is that it is infallible

II. Another characteristic of *the Word of God* is that it is indestructible

III. A third characteristic of the *Word of God* is that it is indispensable

Example:

Subject	Discipleship
Theme	The Cost of Discipleship
Type	Topical
Approach	Characteristics Of
Purpose	To help people realize the cost of discipleship for what it is

Main Divisions:

I. One characteristic of *the cost of discipleship* is that it is expensive

II. Another characteristic of *the cost of discipleship* is that it is painful

III. A third characteristic of *the cost of discipleship* is that it is fearful

Take a look at the following themes and create your own topical message using the "characteristics of" approach. I think you will find that if you discipline yourself to use them you will appreciate their simplicity and advantage.

The Word of God

The Prince of Life

The Path of Life

The Wages of Sin

The Second Coming

The Prince of the Power of the Air

A Servant of the Lord

The Cost of Discipleship   The Narrow Way of
The Deceitfulness of Sin   Salvation

THE "ADVANTAGES IN" APPROACH

The "advantages in" approach is another mechanical device that will enable you to derive main divisions from the theme. Unlike the "characteristics of" approach which describes the essential quality or nature of something, the "advantages in" approach tells us the benefits or favorable results that emerge from a thing. Let's compare the two approaches. For space's sake we will temporarily drop some of the formalities.

Example:

Theme   The Fruit of the Spirit
Approach   Characteristics Of

Main Divisions:

I. One characteristic of *the fruit of the Spirit* is that it is essential
II. Another characteristic of *the fruit of the Spirit* is that it is diverse
III. A third characteristic of *the fruit of the Spirit* is that it is supernatural

Now, the "Advantages In" approach

Example:

I. One advantage of *the fruit of the Spirit* is that by *the fruit of the Spirit* believers enjoy unhindered fellowship with God
II. Another advantage of *the fruit of the Spirit* is that by *the fruit of the Spirit* believers are set free from the works of the flesh

III. A third advantage of *the fruit of the Spirit* is that by *the fruit of the Spirit* believers clearly distinguish the difference between what God does and what man does

In the "characteristics of" approach we are describing the very nature of the fruit of the Spirit. What is it? It is supernatural, it is diverse, it is necessary, it is wonderful, it is spiritual, it is divine, it is gracious, etc. We have told you what it is but we haven't told you specifically what its benefits are. Yes, it is wonderful but how? For example, it benefits us by helping us distinguish between the power of God and our own strength. It benefits us by making our fellowship with God beautiful. It benefits us by causing harmony between believers, etc. The list could go on and on.

Example:

Subject	Holiness
Theme	The Holiness of God
Type	Topical
Approach	Advantages In
Purpose	To help people appreciate (realize the value of) The Holiness of God

Main Divisions:

I. One advantage of *the Holiness of God* is that by *the Holiness of God* sinners are convicted of their sin

II. A second advantage of *the Holiness of God* is that by *the Holiness of God* believers have the assurance that they will see God

III. A third advantage of *the Holiness of God* is that by *the Holiness of God* believers enjoy close communion with God

In each of the above points, conviction of sin, the assurance of seeing God, and enjoying close communion with God, all state the advantages or benefits that accrue from the *Holiness of God*. They are not characteristics or qualities. They are blessings that flow from it. When deciding upon your topical approach you must keep in mind what you want to do. While these approaches may seem very restrictive for the present once you have mastered *Thematic Preaching* the possibilities will be limitless.

Rules of Thumb Regarding "Advantages In"

1. "Characteristics of" approach is looking for an adjective. That is, one word. With "advantages in," however, **entire sentences are possible** when expressing the favorable result.
2. **Themes which express action are a little easier in stating their benefits.** For example, *The Resurrection of Christ, Salvation of the Lost, and Justification by Faith* are all themes that contain some form of action. The above two examples I gave, *The Fruit of the Spirit* and *The Holiness of God,* do not express action but as you can see you can still use them.
3. **Express your advantages as actual, not potential.** Using the theme *Justification by Faith* as an example, a benefit is that believers *are* forgiven. Not, believers *can be* forgiven. Leave the

uncertainty out and state the fact, the real blessing that comes as a result.

4. **Make sure you actually express the favorable results of something. Avoid anything that is not a benefit.** For example, one advantage of *The Spirit of God* is that He is the third member of the trinity. Is that an advantage? Being a member of the trinity is a matter of fact. It is not a benefit that accrues from Him. Here's another example: One advantage of *Pot Holes in the Road* is that by *Pot Holes in the Road* you pop your tires. Is popping your tires an advantage? Certainly not so be careful when you express your benefits in your main divisions. The only advantage of *potholes in the road* is that by *pot holes in the road* there is job security for the highway department.

5. **The purpose in the sermon plan is to help you appreciate your theme.** This is what you will have on mind when you make up your main divisions. This is what you intend on informing your listeners about. You are going to help them appreciate your theme because there are benefits that come from it.

6. As you can see in the above examples I **repeat**ed **the theme twice in the main points.** The reason for this is because it reduces the amount of mistakes you will make when expressing your advantages. Certainly you can say, for example, "one advantage to potholes in the road is that there is job security for the highway department." Eventually you will do this each time because repeating the phrase twice will become unnecessary. For now, however,

you should repeat the theme twice to ensure you are actually expressing the benefits of the theme.

Here are some good themes that you should use to practice the "advantages in" approach.

The Damnation of Demons

Praying without Ceasing

Rejoicing in the Lord Always

Justification by Faith Alone

The Sanctification of Believers

Enduring Until the End

The Patience of the Saints

The Good Fight of Faith

Obedience to the Law

The Salvation of the Lost

THE "NECESSITIES FOR" APPROACH

The third approach used for deriving main points from the theme is the "necessities for" approach. The purpose of this approach is to explain why someone needs to do something or why something is imperative. If the purpose of your sermon is anything other than describing why something is necessary then you should not use this approach. Like the first two it has a very specific and limited application. Let's use an example of the theme *The Damnation of Demons*.

Example:

I. One characteristic of the *Damnation of Demons* is that is scriptural

II. Another characteristic of the *Damnation of Demons* is that is severe

III. A third characteristic of the *Damnation of Demons* is that it is swift

Example:

I. One advantage in the *Damnation of Demons* is that by the *Damnation of Demons* the earth gets purified of their presence
II. Another advantage in the *Damnation of Demons* is that by the *Damnation of Demons* God's saints get relief from their harassment
III. A third advantage in the *Damnation of Demons* is that by the *Damnation of Demons* God's power over them is magnified

Example:

Subject	Demons
Theme	The Damnation of Demons
Type	Topical
Approach	Necessities For
Purpose	To help people know why the Damnation of Demons is imperative

Main Divisions:

I. The *Damnation of Demons* is needful first, in order that the earth might be purified of their presence
II. The *Damnation of Demons* is needful second, in order that the saints might be relieved from their harassment
III. The *Damnation of Demons* is needful third, in order that God's power over them might be manifested

After comparing these last two examples you will probably say "What's the difference between the 'advantages in' approach and the 'necessities for' approach"? "They say the same thing!" No, they do not. The "advantages in" approach tells us why it is advantageous or beneficial. For example, it is advantageous for demons to be damned because the earth gets purified. You are telling the congregation that is a benefit for them to be gone. Is it at the same time a necessity? Yes. The three main divisions of the last two examples demonstrate that they can be both advantages and necessities at the same time. This fact is really not surprising. Something that is necessary will often be advantageous as well. They key is that YOU understand what exactly you want to say and that you are consistent in your presentation. Notice the similarities between the two approaches.

Example:

Theme: The Resurrection of Christ
Main Divisions:

- One advantage of the *resurrection of Christ* is that by the *resurrection of Christ* Jesus demonstrated his victory over death
- *The resurrection of Christ* was needful in order that His victory over death might be demonstrated

The same truth appears in both approaches but the emphasis is different. In the first you are telling the audience what benefits accrue from the resurrection of Christ. In the second you are explaining why the resurrection was necessary.

Example:

Theme   Rejoicing in the Lord Always

Main Divisions:

- One advantage to *Rejoicing in the Lord Always* is that by *Rejoicing in the Lord Always* believers demonstrate their love for God
- *Rejoicing in the Lord Always* is needful in order that the love of God might be demonstrated by believers

The resemblance between the two approaches is obvious. The wording is very similar but their purposes are different. That which is an advantage is often necessary as well. While I have taken pains to show the similarities between the two approaches keep in mind that many times that which is advantageous is not a necessity and vice versa. You should not get worried or confused about their similarities. If the intention of your topical sermon is to state the benefits of something then use the "advantages in" approach. If it is to explain why it is necessary then use the "necessities for" approach. Everything else will fall into place. The key is to know the purpose of your message.

Example:

Subject	Judgment
Theme	The Bema Seat of Christ
Type	Topical
Approach	Necessities For
Purpose	To help people know why the *Bema Seat of Christ is necessary*

Main Divisions:

I. *The Bema Seat of Christ* is needful first, in order that each believer might be rewarded for his faithfulness to the Lord

II. *The Bema Seat of Christ* is needful second, in order that each believer might be corrected concerning his Christian walk.

III. *The Bema Seat of Christ* is needful third, in order that a believer's works might be evaluated as to their purity

Example:

Subject	Evil
Theme	Avoiding the Appearance of Evil
Type	Topical
Approach	Necessities For
Purpose	To help people know why *Avoiding the Appearance of Evil is necessary*

Main Divisions:

I. *Avoiding the Appearance of Evil* is necessary first, in order that a believer might be safeguarded from any unforeseen traps

II. *Avoiding the Appearance of Evil* is necessary second, in order that a believer might not be unfairly judged by other believers

III. *Avoiding the Appearance of Evil* is necessary third, in order that a believer might be assured of a good testimony from those without

Rules of Thumb for "Necessities For"

1. **Be clear that your only purpose is to tell why something is imperative.** You are not giving the purpose for something or the reason for something

or the cause for something. You are stressing the necessity of a thing or action. If you want to stress the purpose or cause of a thing then be consistent (parallel) in your main divisions and state the same fact in all of them.

- One purpose for *avoiding the appearance of evil* is, etc.
- One cause for *avoiding the appearance of evil* is, etc.
- One reason for *avoiding the appearance* of evil is, etc.

There is nothing wrong with doing this in your sermon body. You have effectively created your own approach of devising main divisions from your theme. The key is that you remain consistent and parallel with your thoughts. You cannot begin by stating the necessity of something and then change, for example, to its cause. When you do this you will confuse your audience.

2. **Be sure to use the phrase *in order that* in every main division**. This will emphasize the imperative nature of the thing.

3. **Always use the passive voice of the verb when using the "necessities for" approach.** For example, a*voiding the appearance of evil* is necessary in order that a believer <u>might be safeguarded</u>. The passive voice means that the focus is on the action rather than on the subject. In this case the subject, <u>believer</u>, is being safeguarded, that is where the stress is. He is not safeguarding (the emphasis is on what the subject is doing), he is being safeguarded (emphasis is on the action itself instead of on the

subject's actions). An easy way to help you use the passive voice is to use the words <u>might be</u> or <u>may be</u> along with the past participle (safeguarded). Here's a simple formula to use: Subject + finite form of to be + Past Participle. Filling in the blanks we get: Subject (believer) + finite form of verb to be (might be) + past participle (safeguarded). If you don't use the passive voice your main divisions will be confusingly similar to the "advantages in" approach. That is why it is beneficial to use the passive voice with the "necessities for" approach.

Example:

Subject	Bible
Theme	Reading the Bible Daily
Type	Topical
Approach	Necessities For
Purpose	To help people see why *Reading the Bible Daily is imperative*

Main Divisions:

I. *Reading the Bible daily* is needful first, in order that a Christian might be challenged continuously
II. *Reading the Bible daily* is needful second, in order that a Christian might be fed sufficiently
III. *Reading the Bible daily* is needful third, in order that a Christian might be informed scripturally

Here are some other themes that you can practice using the "necessities for" approach.

Loving Tenaciously	Abiding in the Vine
Preaching in Season/Out	Cleansing Oneself from -
Controlling the Tongue	the Filthiness of the Flesh

White Throne Judgment   The Christian's Armor
The Bema Seat of Christ   The Rapture of the
The Judgment of Demons   Church

THE "REQUIREMENTS FOR" APPROACH

The fourth device for mechanically extracting main divisions from the theme is called the "requirements for" approach. By "requirements for" we mean something that is a prerequisite in order to accomplish the truth stated in the theme. In the words of its inventor, Dr. John Benson, *The "requirements for" approach sets forth conditions by which people can 'become' something, 'obtain' something, 'reach' something, 'develop into' something, 'acquire' something, or even (possibly) 'succeed in' something.*[9] Let's use some examples and explore this approach. Before we do we will recapitulate all the approaches we have learned to this point.

Example:

Subject	Sinners
Theme	Friend of Sinners
Type	Topical
Approach	Characteristics Of
Purpose	To help see what a *Friend of Sinners* is

Main Divisions:

    I.   One characteristic of a *Friend of Sinners* is that he is kind

    II. Another characteristic of a *Friend of Sinners* is that he is patient

---

[9] Benson, 27

III. A third characteristic of a *Friend of Sinners* is that he is mature

Leaving off a few of the formalities we will use the other approaches.

Example:

Approach	Advantages In
Purpose	To help people appreciate being a *Friend of Sinners*

Main Divisions:

I. One Advantage to being a *Friend of Sinners* is that by being a *Friend of Sinners* the lost witness genuine love

II. Another advantage to being a *Friend of Sinners* is that by being a *Friend of Sinners* believers become more sincere children of God

III. A third advantage to being a *Friend of Sinners* is that by being a *Friend of Sinners* the unsaved are introduced to the truth of the Gospel

Example:

Approach	Necessities For
Purpose	To help people know why being a *Friend of Sinners* is imperative

Main Divisions:

I. Being a *Friend of Sinners* is necessary first, in order that unbelievers might be saved

II. Being a *Friend of Sinners* is necessary second, in order that believers might be matured

III. Being a *Friend of Sinners* is necessary third, in order that Jesus' example might be followed

Example:

Approach	Requirements For
Purpose	To help people become a *Friend of Sinners*

Main Divisions:

I. One requirement for becoming a *Friend of Sinners* is a humble heart

II. Another requirement for becoming a *Friend of Sinners* is a patient attitude

III. A third requirement for becoming a *Friend of Sinners* is love for the lost

Example:

Subject	Character
Theme	A Blameless Character
Type	Topical
Approach	Requirements For
Purpose	To help people attain unto a *Blameless Character*

Main Divisions:

I. One requirement for having *a blameless character* is a dedication to purity

II. Another requirement for having *a blameless character* is a surrender to the Spirit

III. A third requirement for having *a blameless character* is a repentant heart

Example:

Subject	Prayer
Theme	Answers to Prayer
Type	Topical

Approach   Requirements For
Purpose   To help people receive *Answers to Prayer*

Main Divisions:

  I. One requirement for receiving *answers to prayer* is the confession of sin
  II. Another requirement for receiving *answers to prayer* is unity between husband and wife
  III. A third requirement for receiving *answers to prayer* is unwavering faith

Example:

Subject   Strength
Theme   Being Strong in the Lord
Type   Topical
Approach   Requirements For
Purpose   To help people become *Strong in the Lord*

Main Divisions:

  I. One requirement for *being strong in the Lord* is an unwavering faith
  II. Another requirement for *being strong in the Lord* is undaunted courage
  III. A third requirement for *being strong in the Lord* is unswerving determination

Rules of Thumb for "Requirements For"

1. The "requirements for" approach **sets forth the conditions** by which people can become something, obtain something, reach something, develop into something, acquire something, succeed in something, or even receive something. If you want to become something there are

requirements for accomplishing that task. If you want to achieve something then there are also requirements corresponding to the accomplishment of it. This approach sets forth those conditions.

2. **Depending on the nature of your theme you will have to modify your purpose accordingly.** For example, if your theme is *Teachers of the Word* then your purpose will be to help people <u>become</u> *Teachers of the Word.* If your theme is *answers to prayer* then your purpose will be to help people <u>receive</u> answers to prayer. If your theme is *a blameless character* then your theme will be to help people <u>attain unto</u> a blameless character or <u>to have</u> a blameless character. In each case the purpose statement should accurately reflect the conditions necessary to the accomplishment of your theme.

3. **Be careful not to suggest that people become what they already are or already have.** For example, if your theme is *A Royal Priesthood* it would be theologically incorrect to suggest that believers should become a royal priesthood because they already are. They may not realize it but they are. Likewise, a believer cannot become one with Christ because he already is. He can become closer or appreciate it more but he cannot become what he already is.

4. **Be careful not to use themes which make it impossible to set forth the conditions of something.** For example, with the theme *The Good Shepherd*, how can a believer become the *Good*

Shepherd? This is absurd. There is only one Good Shepherd and no one is able to become Him or attain unto Him. You either have the wrong theme or the wrong approach. You might alter your theme to *The Character of the Good Shepherd.* Then it would make sense to set forth the requirements of obtaining a character like his.

Here are some themes to practice the "Requirements For" approach.

Ambassadors for Christ	Peace of the Lord
Preachers of the Word	Rejoicing in the Lord
Giant Killers	A Pure Heart
Faithfulness in Life	A Clean Conscience
	Examples to the Flock
	The Soul Winner

"DUTIES TOWARD" AND "DUTIES IN" APPROACH

The sixth and seventh mechanical devices used for deriving main divisions from the theme are called the "duties toward" and the "duties in" approaches. These approaches are not used very often but there may be occasions that justify their inclusion here. Just as the "requirements for" approach sets forth the requirements necessary for something so the "duties toward" and "duties in" approaches set forth the duties. For example, with the theme *Missionary Service to the Lord*, one requirement might be a year's training in Bible and evangelism. One duty, however, might be to pray and fast about missionary service to the Lord.

Requirements stress the things necessary for accomplishing the theme but duties stress the responsibilities or obligations toward that theme. It is the duty in missionary service to pray about it. You should not be concerned about confusing the approaches because many duties might also be requirements. If you are stressing the duties of something don't worry about crossing the line by stating a requirement instead. It is where you choose to lay the emphasis. Let's begin by looking at the "duties toward" approach and then we will compare it with the "duties in."

Example:

Subject	Christian Service
Theme	Service in the Local Rescue Mission
Type	Topical
Approach	Duties Toward
Purpose	To help people know what they should do concerning *Service in the Local Rescue Mission*

Main Divisions:

I.   One duty toward *service in the local rescue mission* is to consecrate yourself for *service in the local rescue mission*

II. Another duty toward *service in the local rescue mission* is to pray about *service in the local rescue mission*

III. A third duty toward *service in the local rescue mission* is to learn about *service in the local rescue mission*

Example:

Subject	Scripture
Theme	Interpreting the Scripture
Type	Topical
Approach	Duties Toward
Purpose	To help people know what they should do concerning *Interpreting Scripture*

Main Divisions:

I. One duty toward *interpreting Scripture* is to pray and fast about *interpreting Scripture*
II. Another duty toward *interpreting Scripture* is to educate yourself about *interpreting Scripture*
III. A third duty toward *interpreting Scripture* is to practice *interpreting Scripture*

Example:

Subject	Preaching
Theme	Preaching Evangelistic Messages
Type	Topical
Approach	Duties Toward
Purpose	To help people know what they should do concerning *Preaching Evangelistic Messages*

Main Divisions:

I. One duty toward *preaching evangelistic messages* is to encourage *preaching evangelistic messages*
II. Another duty toward *preaching evangelistic messages* is to desire *preaching evangelistic messages*
III. A third duty toward *preaching evangelistic messages* is to learn about *preaching evangelistic messages*

Rules of Thumb for "Duties For"

1. To keep this approach distinct from "duties in" **only use infinitives after your theme.** For example, one duty toward *interpreting Scripture* is **to practice** *interpreting Scripture*. If you don't use an infinitive you will probably end up stating the "duties in" something rather than the "duties toward" it. Like the other approaches this has a very specific application.
2. **It is absolutely necessary to restate the theme after the infinitive.** For example, one duty toward *interpreting Scripture* is to practice ***interpreting Scripture***. The key to stating the duties 'toward' something is not only to use an infinitive after stating the theme but also to restate the theme after the infinitive. If you don't adhere to these two rules steadfastly you will either state the duties 'in' something or you will state the means by which something occurs.
3. **Learn the difference between the *duties toward* something and the *duties in* something.** For example, using the theme *Being a Good Witness for the Lord* one duty toward it would be to pray

about *being a good witness,* or to learn how to *be a good witness for the Lord.* These are duties toward it but they are not duties in it. A duty in it would be the duty of passing out tracts or the duty of street preaching. Using the theme *The Deacon Ministry* as another example one duty in *the deacon ministry* is the duty of ushering. Another duty in the *deacon ministry* is the duty of passing out the elements. These are duties in it but they are not duties toward it. Each of these approaches has specific applications and you should know the difference. If you are not sure stick to the formula above (theme, infinitive, theme) and you will be stating the duties toward the theme. If the formula does not work then your desire is probably to state the duties in the theme. Neither is right or wrong, it is what you want to say.

Example: Duties In

Subject	Ministry
Theme	Music Ministry
Type	Topical
Approach	Duties In
Purpose	To help people know what their duties in Music Ministry are

Main Divisions:

I.   One duty in *the music ministry* is the duty of organizing a worship team
II. Another duty in *the music ministry* is the duty of leading congregational singing
III. A third duty in *the music ministry* is the duty of conducting a children's choir

Example:

Subject	Evangelism
Theme	Soul winning
Type	Topical
Approach	Duties In
Purpose	To help people know what their duties in *Soul Winning* are

Main Divisions:

I. One duty in *soul winning* is the duty of street preaching

II. Another duty in *soul winning* is the duty of door-to-door evangelism

III. A third duty in *soul winning* is the duty of organizing a visitation team

It may seem confusing to keep these two related approaches separate but it will help clarify your purpose if you do. The more coherent your theme is the more logical your sermon becomes. People in the pew are waiting to hear something that interests them. Often they never get it. By being consistent and parallel with your thoughts they will know for certain that you have a specific message for them. If your thoughts are confused they may leave thinking that you were not certain about what you wanted to say.

Rules of Thumb for "Duties In"

1. **Be sure to state "duties in" in every main division.** For example, one **duty in** *soul winning,* etc. This will ensure you are giving the duties in something and not the duties toward it.

2. For caution's sake state **"duties" again after the verb.** For example, one duty in *soul winning* is **the duty of,** etc. This will help you specify your purpose: To give the specific responsibilities associated with *soul winning*.

3. **The duties you give should be easily recognizable as pertaining to responsibilities of the theme.** There should be no confusion. This approach is very simple. For example, one duty of *soul winning* is street preaching, another is door-to-door evangelism, and another is organizing an evangelistic team. Each of these duties is a responsibility **in** the task of *soul winning*.

4. Themes that express action have duties in them but themes that do not express action may not. For safety's sake **use themes that express action.**

Practice Themes: "Duties Toward" & "Duties In"

Walking in the Light	Spiritual – Stewardship
Praying without Ceasing	Forgiving - Offenses
Ministering to the Lonely	Praising – Continuously
Redeeming the Time	Ministering as a Deacon
Counting the Cost	Mortifying the Flesh
Biblical Tithing	
Giving Generously	

THE "MANNER OF" APPROACH

The eighth mechanical device used to extract main divisions from the theme is called the "manner of" approach. This device sets forth the manner in which something happens. *It is the way or mode and answers the question of HOW an event occurs.*[10] It is fairly easy to use because the word "manner" implies an adverb. Take a look at its simplicity.

Example:

Subject	Justification
Theme	Justification by Grace through Faith
Type	Topical
Approach	Manner Of
Purpose	To help people understand how Justification by Grace through Faith occurs

Main Divisions:

    I. *Justification by Grace through faith* occurs unconditionally

    II. *Justification by Grace through faith* occurs supernaturally

    III. *Justification by Grace through faith* occurs mercifully

Example:

Theme	The Salvation of the Lost

Main Divisions:

    I. *The Salvation of the Lost* occurs prayerfully

---

[10] Benson, 44.

II. *The Salvation of the Lost* occurs intentionally

III. *The Salvation of the Lost* occurs supernaturally

Example:

Theme   Effective Bible Reading

Main Divisions:

  I. *Effective Bible Reading* occurs regularly
  II. *Effective Bible Reading* occurs patiently
  III. *Effective Bible Reading* occurs spiritually

Each of these examples tells how the theme comes to pass. That is, regularly, patiently, and spiritually, etc. The adverbs mark the ways each theme occurs. You should keep the format simple as in the above cases. Do not think simplicity is a sign of weakness. Remember the rule of thumb regarding themes from chapter two: **The simpler the theme is the easier it is to preach and the easier it is for the listeners to follow.** It is usually better, therefore, if themes are stated in the simplest manner possible. In the same fashion keep this approach simple and you are likely to convey thoughts that the audience will successfully follow. Due to the elementary nature of this approach it is easy to state the main divisions in another way.

Example:

Theme   The Presentation of the Gospel

Purpose   To help people understand how the
               Presentation of the Gospel occurs

Main Divisions:

  I. *The Gospel is presented* tactfully
  II. *The Gospel is presented* graciously
  III. *The Gospel is presented* biblically

Example:

Theme   The Creation of the Universe
Main Divisions:

   I. The *creation* *of* *the* *universe* occurred instantaneously
  II. The *creation of the universe* occurred intentionally
 III. The *creation of the universe* occurred intelligently

Example:

Theme   The Rapture of the Church
Main Divisions:

   I. *The rapture of the church* will occur imminently
  II. *The rapture of the church* will occur discriminately
 III. *The rapture of the church* will occur powerfully

Rules of Thumb for "Manner Of"

1. **Because you are describing the manner in which something occurs you must use an adverb!** Do not take liberties and use any other part of speech. This approach will also be useful when preparing expository sermons. Besides the "characteristics of" approach this may be the most used of the approaches thus far.
2. **The themes you choose will most likely express some form of action due to the fact that you are using adverbs to describe them.** For example, *the rapture of the church, the creation of the universe, the presentation of the Gospel,* all depict action. Keep this in mind as you choose your theme. Themes such as *The Bread of* Life are not conducive to use in this method. How can *The Bread of Life*

occur? This is an absurdity. *The Bread of life* is a person, The Lord Jesus Christ. He does not occur. He is. If you cannot use this approach easily then it is probably the wrong one for your theme.

3. **Your purpose is to help people understand how the theme occurs.** When you write out your sermon plan you should state it this way. If you take pains to do this there will be no mistaking what you intend to accomplish. You are helping people understand how the theme occurs.

Here are some themes that you can use to practice this approach.

Forgiving the Offense of a Brother	The Salvation of a Lost Soul
Proper Stewardship	The Giving of the Law
The Spiritual Discipline of Fasting	The Beginning of the Church
Celebration of the Lord's Table	The Spirit-Filled Life
Anti-Christ's Destruction	The Practice of Godliness

THE "ACTUALITIES OF" APPROACH

This approach (as well as the next one) dates back to the founder of *Thematic Preaching*, Dr. Gordon C. Davis. Dr. Kroll includes this in his book <u>The Prescription for Preaching</u> as an approach used to prove something. He says:

The "actualities of" approach is designed to prove that the theme is true. In this method we are not attempting to teach men something but to convince them of something. Thus, it is vitally important that words like fact and proof be used throughout. It is our purpose to convince men of the reality of the theme.[11]

Example:

Subject	Judgment
Theme	Joshua's Destruction of the Canaanite Cities in Palestine
Type	Topical
Approach	Actualities Of (The Proving Approach)
Purpose	To bring men to believe in the fact of *Joshua's Destruction*

Main Divisions:

    I. One proof of *the destruction of the Canaanite cities in Palestine* is the fact that the inerrant Word of God declares it

    II. Another proof of *the destruction of the Canaanite cities in Palestine* is the fact that archeological digs have verified it

    III. Another proof of *the destruction of the Canaanite cities in Palestine* is the fact that ancient civilizations have recorded it

Example:

Subject	Salvation
Theme	A Free Salvation
Type	Topical
Approach	Actualities Of
Purpose	To bring men to believe in the fact that *Salvation is Free*

Main Divisions:

---

[11] Kroll, 201.

I. One proof that *salvation is free* is the fact that Jesus said it was free
II. Another proof that *salvation is free* is the fact that personal experience testifies to its freedom
III. A third proof that *salvation is free* is the fact that logic insists that it is free

Rules of Thumb for "Actualities Of"

1. Remember that **this approach is used specifically to prove that the theme is true.** No other purpose is possible.
2. Remember to **use words like *fact* and *proof* in your main divisions.** If you get sloppy and forget to do so you will eventually do something other than to prove that your theme is true. When this happens you will confuse your audience.
3. **The purpose of your sermon is to bring men to believe that your theme is true.** Be sure to remember this as you create your main divisions and remember to write out the entire sermon plan with the purpose clearly stated and understood.

Here are some themes that you can use to practice the "actualities of" approach.

The Resurrection of Christ

Miracles in the Bible

The Infallibility of Scripture

The Presence of the Spirit

The Assurance of God's Forgiveness

The Raising of Lazarus from the Dead

The Deity of Christ

The Love of God

Noah's Worldwide Flood

The Parting of the Red Sea

THE "ADVISABILITY" APPROACH

This approach attempts to convince men why something is advisable and is the best mechanical device for bringing men to a decision making point. While the other approaches can accomplish the same thing the "advisability of" is designed specifically for that purpose. *You are inspiring Christians to receive, gain, choose, do, accomplish, perform, or become the theme.* [12] It is considered an approach of arousal that inspires men to take action.

Example:

Subject	Armor
Theme	Putting on the Armor of God
Type	Topical
Approach	Advisability Of
Purpose	Urging men to decide that *Putting on the Armor of God is Advisable*

Main Divisions:

I. *Putting on the armor of God* is advisable, first, because Scripture warns us that we are in a spiritual war

II. *Putting on the armor of God* is advisable, second, because Great men of God always wore theirs

III. *Putting on the armor of God* is advisable, third, because wearing it gives us a sense of confidence in the fight

---

[12] Kroll, 209.

Example:

Subject   Souls
Theme   Winning Lost Souls
Type   Topical
Approach   Advisability Of

Purpose   To urge men to decide that *Winning Lost*
               Souls is advisable

Main Divisions:

I. *Winning lost souls* is advisable, first, because Proverbs tell us it is wise to do so

II. *Winning lost souls* is advisable, second, because it pleases our Lord

III. *Winning lost souls* is advisable, third, because the need of men is so great

Rules of Thumb for "Advisability Of"

1. Remember that **this topical sermon approach stresses why something is advisable, hence, it encourages a decision.** It is an approach of arousing men to action. If the purpose of your sermon is not to encourage a decision then you are using the wrong approach.

2. **Your choice of themes must reflect the idea that you are striving for a decision.** For example, if you use the theme, *Jesus, The Good Shepherd,* you cannot use this approach. How can you state the advisability of *the Good Shepherd*? You can state the advisability of *knowing* Him but you cannot state the advisability *of* Him.

3. **Always use the term "advisable" in your main divisions.** This will keep you on track so that you

don't stray and emphasize something other than why people should consider the idea contained in the theme.

Here are some themes you can use to practice this sermon approach.

The Use of Spiritual Gifts	Daily Bible Reading
To Pray Without Ceasing	Living Holy Lives
Rejoicing Always	Coming Boldly to the
Encouraging One Another	Throne of Grace
Caring for the Flock	Proper Spiritual
To Disciple New Believers	Leadership

THE "ASPECTS OF" APPROACH

Of all the approaches for topical sermons we have studied so far the "aspects of" is without question the most beneficial and versatile. Its value cannot be overstated on account of its flexibility and versatility. Besides these shining qualities it serves the basis for the expository method of preaching. This alone is enough to warrant its accolades.

Let's recap the mechanical devices we have already studied and then dive into the "aspects of" approach. We will use the theme *The Salvation of Lost Souls* and drop some of the formalities for time's sake.

Example:

Theme   The Salvation of Lost Souls
Approach   Characteristics Of
Main Divisions:

I. One characteristic of *the salvation of lost souls* is that it is merciful
II. Another characteristic of *the salvation of lost souls* is that it is magnificent
III. A third characteristic of *the salvation of lost souls* is that it is mighty

Example:

Approach   Advantages In
Main Divisions:

I. One advantage of *the salvation of lost souls* is that by *the salvation of lost souls* sinners will escape the judgment of God
II. Another advantage of *the salvation of lost souls* is that by *the salvation of lost souls* God's love is demonstrated to a dying world
III. Another advantage of *the salvation of lost souls* is that by *the salvation of lost souls* sinners have hope for the future

Example:

Approach   Necessities For
Main Divisions:

I.   *The salvation of lost souls* is needful first, in order that sinners might be delivered from impending hell
II.   The salvation of lost souls is needful second, in order that the mercy of God might be exhibited to a dying world
III.   *The salvation of lost souls* is needful third, in order that the Scriptures might be fulfilled

Example:

Approach   Requirements For
Main Divisions:

   I.   One requirement for *the salvation of lost souls* is a conviction by the Holy Spirit

   II. Another requirement for *the salvation of lost* souls is a consecration to the will of God

  III. A third requirement of *the salvation of lost souls* is a commitment to the truth of Scripture

Example:

Approach   Duties Toward
Main Divisions:

   I.   One duty toward *the salvation of lost souls* is to pray for *the salvation of lost souls*

   II. Another duty toward *the salvation of lost souls* is to prepare for *the salvation of lost souls*

  III. A third duty toward *the salvation of lost souls* is to participate in *the salvation of lost souls*

Example:

Approach   Duties In
Main Divisions:

   I.   One duty in *the salvation of lost souls* is the duty of preaching the Gospel

   II. Another duty in *the salvation of lost souls* is the duty of passing out tracts

  III. A third duty in *the salvation of lost souls* is the duty of personal soul winning

Example:

Approach   Manner Of
Main Divisions:

I. *The salvation of lost souls* occurs miraculously
II. *The salvation of lost souls* occurs mercifully
III. *The salvation of lost souls* occurs methodically

Example:

Approach   Actualities Of
Main Divisions:

I. One proof of *the salvation of lost souls* is the fact that converts testify to their changes lives
II. Another proof of *the salvation of lost souls* is the fact that the inerrant Word of God declares it
III. A third proof of *the salvation of lost souls* is the fact that Jesus' death secured it

Example:

Approach   Advisability Of
Main Divisions:

I. *The salvation of lost souls* is advisable first, because the punishment for sin is so terrible
II. *The salvation of lost souls* is advisable second, because the life styles of sinners is so painful
III. *The salvation of lost souls* is advisable third, because it fulfills the Great Commission

The Prefix Form of the "Aspects Of" Approach

Finally, let's look at the full sermon plan using the "aspects of" approach. The "aspects of" approach has four ways expressing the aspects of the theme. We will begin using the "prefix form." We call this the "prefix" form because the qualifying noun is placed before the theme as the following examples demonstrate.

Example:

Subject   Salvation
Theme   The Salvation of Lost Souls
Type   Topical
Approach   Aspects of/Prefix form
Purpose   To help people know about the *Salvation of Lost Souls*

Main Divisions:

I. One aspect of *the salvation of lost souls* is the method of *the salvation of lost souls*

II. Another aspect of *the salvation of lost souls* is the need for *the salvation of lost souls*

III. A third aspect of *the salvation of lost souls* is the reward of *the salvation of lost souls*

The above sermon plan demonstrates what the "aspects of" approach does. It delineates aspects of the theme. How many aspects are there to *the salvation of lost souls*? Perhaps hundreds. To put the usefulness of this approach into perspective let's devise more main divisions using the same theme *The Salvation of Lost Souls.*

Example:

1. One aspect of *the salvation of lost souls* is the **characteristics of** *the salvation of lost souls*

2. Another aspect of *the salvation of lost souls* is the **advantages in** *the salvation of lost souls*

3. A third aspect of *the salvation of lost souls* is the **necessity for** *the salvation of lost souls*

4. A fourth aspect of *the salvation of lost souls* is the **requirements for** *the salvation of lost souls*
5. A fifth aspect of *the salvation of lost souls* is the **duties toward** *the salvation of lost souls*
6. A sixth aspect of *the salvation of lost souls* is the **duties in** *the salvation of lost souls*
7. A seventh aspect of *the salvation of lost souls* is the **manner of** *the salvation of lost souls*
8. An eighth aspect of *the salvation of lost* souls is the **actualities of** *the salvation of lost souls*
9. A final aspect of *the salvation of lost souls* is the **advisability of** *the salvation of lost souls*

Since we have already devised main divisions from each of these sermon plans do you think we have enough information to preach about *The Salvation of Lost Souls*? This is why the "aspects of" approach is the most common and versatile of all the mechanical devices. You should know, however, that its versatility goes beyond using the other sermon approaches as main divisions. You can use any aspect of the theme you choose. There are no limits.

Essentially, the "aspects of" approach qualifies the theme in some respect. It narrows or restricts it so that a particular aspect of it is treated as a main division. Using the theme, for example, *The Rapture of the Church* we can restrict it to the *time* of the Rapture of the Church, the *importance* of the Rapture of the Church, or the *scriptural support* for the Rapture of the Church, etc. In each case a different aspect of the theme is presented as a main division. The amount of aspects available to any theme is staggering. The versatility of this approach, therefore, is without par. Not only will a preacher's sermon remain coherent (due to the fact that the same theme is repeated in every main division) but his flexibility in handling the theme is limitless. *Thematic Preaching* is the most logical system of homiletics ever created. As we study the expository method of preparing sermons we will discover that *Thematic Preaching* naturally traces the literary flow of the biblical text.

Example:

Subject	Preaching
Theme	Preaching Thematic Sermons
Type	Topical
Approach	Aspects Of
Purpose	To help people know about *Preaching Thematic Sermons*

Main Divisions:

I. One aspect *of preaching thematic sermons* is the ease of *preaching thematic sermons*
II. Another aspect of *preaching thematic sermons* is the flexibility of *preaching thematic sermons*
III. A third aspect of *preaching thematic sermons* is the coherence in *preaching thematic sermons*

Example:

Subject	The Holy Spirit
Theme	The Spirit-Filled Life
Type	Topical
Approach	Aspects Of
Purpose	To help people know about *The Spirit-Filled Life*

Main Divisions:

I. One aspect of *the Spirit-filled life* is the source of *the Spirit-filled life*
II. Another aspect of *the Spirit-filled life* is the sacredness of the Spirit-filled life
III. A third aspect of *the Spirit-filled life* is the seriousness of *the Spirit-filled life*

Devising Subpoints From Main Points

Now let's devise subpoints from main divisions using our previous approaches. We will begin with the theme *A Surrendered Life.*

Example:

Subject   Surrender
Theme   A Surrendered Life
Type   Topical
Approach   Aspects Of
Purpose   To help people know more about *A Surrendered Life*

Main Divisions:

I. One aspect of *a surrendered life* is the necessity for *a surrendered life*
   1. *A surrendered life* is needful first, in order that a believer might be delivered from the tyranny of his own appetites
   2. *A surrendered life* is needful second, in order that God's will might be fully understood
   3. *A surrendered life* is needful third, in order that the power of the Spirit might be totally released

II.   Another aspect of *a surrendered life* is the characteristics of *a surrendered life*
1. One characteristic of *a surrendered life* is that it is peaceful
2. Another characteristic of *a surrendered life* is that it is patient
3. A third characteristic of *a surrendered life* is that it is priceless

III.   A third aspect of *a surrendered life* is the requirements for *a surrendered life*
1. One requirement for *a surrendered life* is a humble heart
2. Another requirement for *a surrendered life* is a trust in His love
3. A third requirement for *a surrendered life* is a disdain for this world

Thus we have created a topical sermon packed with spiritual truth using a total of four of our approaches.

Example:

Subject	Spiritual War
Theme	The War between the Flesh and the Spirit
Type	Topical
Approach	Aspects Of
Purpose	To help people know more about *The War Between the Flesh and the Spirit*

Main Divisions:

I.   One aspect of *the war between the flesh and the Spirit* are the duties toward the war

1. One duty toward *the war between the flesh and the Spirit* is to prepare for the war
2. Another duty toward *the war between the flesh and the Spirit* is to pray and fast about the war
3. Another duty toward *the war between the flesh and the Spirit* is to participate in the war

II. Another aspect of *the war between the flesh and the Spirit* is the manner of the war
   1. *The war* occurs intensely
   2. *The war* occurs intentionally
   3. *The war* occurs imminently

III. A third aspect of *the war between the flesh and the Spirit* are the advantages of *the war*
   1. One advantage of *the war between the flesh and the Spirit* is that by *the war* believers learn to appreciate the value of their salvation
   2. Another advantage of *the war between the flesh and the Spirit* is that by *the war* people learn to fear God more
   3. A third advantage of *the war between the flesh and the Spirit* is that by *the war* unbelievers learn to repent more sincerely

Creating Sub, Subpoints

We have devised a sermon chockfull of spiritual truth. In reality it would be very difficult to do justice to these last two sermon outlines on account of the vast information they contain. Before proceeding further it is a good time to demonstrate how easy it is to create sub, subpoints using the other mechanical devices as well. Let me demonstrate using number II in the example above *The manner of the war between the flesh and the Spirit.*

Example:

Sub-Divisions:

1. The war occurs intensely (We will now use the "characteristics of" approach so we must restate the theme as *The Characteristics of the Intense War*)
    1) One characteristic of *the intense war* is that it is costly
    2) Another characteristic of *the intense war* is that it is cruel
    3) A third characteristic of *the intense war* is that it is continuous
2. The war occurs intentionally (*The duties In the Intentional War*)
    1) One duty in *the intentional war* is the duty of girding up the loins of your mind
    2) Another duty in *the intentional war* is the duty of fleeing youthful lusts
    3) A third duty in *the intentional war* is the duty of putting on the armor of God
3. The war occurs imminently *(The Aspects of the Imminent War)*
    1) One aspect of the *imminent (or eventual) war* is the enemies in the imminent war
    2) Another aspect of *the imminent war* is the emotion of the *imminent war*
    3) A third aspect of *the imminent war* is the end of *the imminent war*

Let's recap what we have just devised in the above example and explore how to create subpoints while keeping the sermon brief and uncomplicated. Our theme is *The War between the Flesh and the Spirit.*

II. One aspect of that *war* is the manner of the *war*
1. The *war occurs intensely*
1) One characteristic of *the intense war* is that it is costly

The major division is number **II.** The sub point is **1.** The sub, subpoint is **1).** Notice that when we progressed through the sermon plan from subpoint to sub, subpoint the theme had to be altered slightly. We went from *The War Occurs Intensely* to *One Characteristic of the Intense War.* We had to turn the adverb into an adjective so it would work with the "characteristics of" approach. You should make this change in your sermon plan so that you keep your thoughts clear. When you deliver the message, however, you can flow rather easily through the changes from point to subpoint to sub, subpoint. This is how naturally the wording of your sermon should flow:

One aspect of the war between the flesh and the Spirit is the manner of the war. That is, the war occurs intensely. In addition, one characteristic of this intense war is that it is costly.

Obviously, this is abbreviated greatly but the point is clear. The logical progression of thoughts will not throw the audience off track. They should easily follow your reasoning. It helps, however, to write out the entire sermon plan and make the changes with pen and ink. Then, practice verbally how the transition takes place. Each subpoint of the outline is a further qualification of the theme. In other words the theme gets restricted each time you create another subpoint. As you progress from point to subpoint the theme will be restricted (or another aspect of it expressed) and will need to be altered accordingly. If the progression from point to subpoint does not flow naturally then you probably made a mistake along the way and you need to correct it before you deliver the message. Below is an example of what your sermon plan should look like in your study:

I. The war occurs intensely: *The Characteristics of the Intense War*
   1. One characteristic of *the intense war* is that it is costly
   2. Another characteristic of *the intense war* is that it is cruel
   3. A third characteristic of *the intense war* is that it is continuous

Your audience will neither know nor care what your sermon plan looks like. The point is that your thought progression remains logical so they can follow. As you restate the theme from *The War Occurs Intensely* to *The Characteristics of the Intense War* the shift in wording should not confuse anyone. The phrase *occurring intensely* means the same thing as *the intense war*. As I stated earlier the details of the sermon plan should remain in the study. The only concern of the listeners is that your sermon makes sense.

You now have at your disposal the means to create main divisions, subdivisions, and sub, subdivisions. Armed with this knowledge you will be able to create complete topical messages that your audience will be able to understand and apply. You have a tried and true homiletical method so that when you are preparing topical sermons you will not view it as an overwhelming task.

The "Aspects of" Approach and the Expository Method

The purpose of these examples is to show you the logic and ease of preparing topical sermons. As I stated before the "aspects of" approach also lays the ground work for the expository method of preaching. Let's use the example given in chapter four of this book *Choosing a theme from the three sermon types: The message to the Church at Ephesus.* Here's the biblical text:

Example: Revelation 2:1-7

Unto the angel of the church of Ephesus write; These things saith he that holdeth the seven stars in his right hand, who walketh in the midst of the seven golden candlesticks; 2 I know thy works, and thy labour, and thy patience, and how thou canst not bear them which are evil: and thou hast tried them which say they are apostles, and are not, and hast found them liars: 3 And hast borne, and hast patience, and for my name's sake hast laboured, and hast not fainted. 4 Nevertheless I have somewhat against thee, because thou hast left thy first love. 5 Remember therefore from whence thou art fallen, and repent, and do the first works; or else I will come unto thee quickly, and will remove thy candlestick out of his place, except thou repent. 6 But this thou hast, that thou hatest the deeds of the Nicolaitanes, which I also hate. 7 He that hath an ear, let him hear what the Spirit saith unto the churches; To him that overcometh will I give to eat of the tree of life, which is in the midst of the paradise of God.

Subject	The Church
Theme	The Message to the Church at Ephesus
Type	Topical & Expository
Approach	Aspects Of
Purpose	To help people know about *The Message to the Church at Ephesus*

Main Divisions:

I.   The Captain of the Church (1)
II.   The Commendation to the Church (2,3,6)
III.   The Correction of the Church (4)
IV.   The Caution to the Church (5)
V.   The Counsel to the Church (7)

All of these main divisions are aspects of the theme *the Message to the Church at Ephesus.* One aspect is the Captain (or commander) of the Church found in verse 1. Another aspect is the Commendation (praises) to the church found in verses 2, 3, and 6. The rest of the aspects can easily be traced as you read the rest of the text. In addition each of these main divisions contains many other aspects that serve as possibilities for subpoints depending upon where the preacher wants to go. This is not the time to discuss the expository method of preaching. We will handle that in detail later. From the above example, however, you can see the logical development of theme made possible through the "aspects of" approach.

The Suffix Form of the "Aspects Of" Approach

Before going further let's look at an alternate way of expressing the "aspects of" approach. In the above examples the qualifying aspect is always placed before the theme. For example using the theme, T*he Rapture of the Church*, we would qualify it as *The Time of the Rapture of the Church.* Dr. John Benson called this the "prefix form" of the "aspects of" device. This is the most common method for this approach. There is another option, however, which Dr. Benson called the "suffix form." In contrast to the prefix form the "suffix form" places the qualifying aspect after the theme with this method.

Example:

Theme   The Call of God
Main Divisions:

I.   One aspect of *the call of God* is *the call of God* to Old Testament Prophets
II. Another aspect of *the call of God* is *the call of God* to the Apostles
III. A third aspect of *the call of God* is *the call of God* to Church Saints

Example:

Theme   The Preaching of the Gospel
Main Divisions:

I.   One aspect of *the preaching of the Gospel* is *the preaching of the Gospel* by Jesus to Nicodemus
II. Another aspect of *the preaching of the Gospel* is *the preaching of the Gospel* by Paul to the Athenians
III. A third aspect of *the preaching of the Gospel* is *the preaching of the Gospel* by Peter to Cornelius

Example:

Theme   Messianic Prophesies
Main Divisions:

I.   One aspect of *Messianic prophecies* is *Messianic prophesies* predicted
II. Another aspect of *Messianic prophecies* is *Messianic prophesies* presented
III. A third aspect of *Messianic prophecies* is *Messianic prophesies* promoted

The purpose of showing you this second choice for the "aspects of" approach is so that you appreciate the flexibility of word usage as you devise your main points. This particular mechanical device allows you a great amount of leeway in order to logically state your divisions in a parallel fashion.

The Enumerative Form of the "Aspects Of" Approach

A third form of the "aspects of" approach is available to you in case the occasion arises. It is called the "enumerative" form and is used when you are working with a plural theme. As its name suggests you are enumerating the contents of the theme. For example using the theme, *Great Women of Prayer*, your divisions might look like this: One woman of prayer was Hannah. Another woman of prayer was Deborah. A third woman of prayer was Rebecca, etc. Notice that these divisions do not use the phrase "aspect of" in them. They are, in fact, aspects of the theme but to use that specific wording makes the English awkward. Once you become familiar with *Thematic Preaching* you will have more liberty to express your divisions freely and consistently without losing your parallelism. The enumerative form of the "aspects of" approach simply lists the parts into numerical order. Remember that you must use a plural theme with this approach. A singular theme cannot be enumerated.

Example:

Theme   The Parables of Our Lord
Main Divisions:

    I.   One *parable of the Lord* is the parable of the sower and the seed

II. Another *parable of the Lord* is the parable of the 10 virgins

III. A third *parable of the Lord* is the parable of the wheat and tares

Example:

Theme   The Fruit of the Spirit
Main Divisions:

I. One *fruit of the Spirit* is the fruit of love
II. Another *fruit of the Spirit* is the fruit of joy
III. A third *fruit of the Spirit* is the fruit of peace

The Comparative Form of the "Aspects Of" Approach

Before ending this discussion there is one more form of the "aspects of" approach which will be very helpful as you are faced with the challenges associated with stating your main divisions. Dr. Benson called it the "comparative" form. Essentially, the comparative form can be likened to a mathematical equation wherein one side of the equation must be balanced with the other. In the equation $x = y$, whatever the value of x is must be equal to y. The comparative form acts the same way.

Example:

Theme   The Parables of Jesus
Main Divisions:

I. *The parables of Jesus* are evidences of his divine wisdom
II. *The parables of Jesus* are expressions of his heavenly calling
III. *The parables of Jesus* are exhortations of his Kingly authority

In each of these main divisions *The Parables of Jesus* are equated with a value: Divine wisdom, a heavenly calling, and kingly authority. One side of the equation is compared or equated to the other.

Example:

Theme   The Gifts of the Spirit
Main Divisions:

I. *The gifts of the Spirit* are proofs of God's love
II. *The gifts of the Spirit* are promises of Divine enablement
III. *The gifts of the Spirit* are presentations of heavenly power

Example:

Theme   The Judgment of God
Main Divisions:

I. *The judgment of God* is a promise of His vindication
II. *The judgment of God* is a prevention of sin's continuance
III. *The judgment of God* is a promotion of His righteousness

Rules of Thumb For "Aspects Of"

1. The most important thing to understand about the "aspects of" is that **when you are creating main divisions all you are doing is qualifying the theme in order to preach about a different aspect of it.** For example with the theme *The Resurrection of Christ* you could qualify it to *The Time of the Resurrection, The Circumstances of the Resurrection*, etc.

2. **Remember that each theme has countless aspects to it.** There are no limits. It is for this reason this approach is so useful.

3. **Keep in mind that not only does the prefix form yield the aspects of the theme, but also the suffix form** (qualifying aspect appears after the theme), **the enumerative form** (takes the plural theme and makes the main divisions out of the individuals), **and the comparative form** (theme is compared to or analogized with a corresponding truth), **are still aspects of the theme.**

4. **Remember that you can make subpoints from the main divisions by using the other approaches.** For example, ***Theme:*** *California Redwoods*. ***Main Division***: One ***characteristic of*** *California Redwoods* is that they are tall. ***Sub Division***: One ***proof*** that the *California Redwoods* are tall is the fact that their linear length is the longest of any other species of trees.

5. **If you make more divisions out of the sub-divisions using the other approaches your theme will be adapted in order that your new divisions flow naturally.** For example:

    - Main Division: One characteristic of *California Redwoods* is that they are tall
    - Sub Division: One proof that *California Redwoods* are tall is the fact that their linear length is the longest of all trees
    - Sub, Subdivision: One duty toward proving that *California Redwoods* are tall is to calibrate the measuring device regularly.

Thus we have at our disposal a total of ten approaches or mechanical devices that will enable you to extract main divisions from your theme. In addition you also have the ability to create subdivisions from your main points using the approaches. If none of the approaches are suitable for your theme you at least have learned the nature of *Thematic Preaching* and will be able to state your main divisions in a logical and parallel fashion. Before going on to our next section here are some themes you can practice using the "aspects of" approach.

The Pride of Life	The Wiles of the Devil
Joy in the Lord	The Choice of Happiness
A Peculiar People	The Prayers of Paul
Struggles Against Sin	Genuine Repentance
A Heart for the Lost	The Wisdom of Silence
The Sin of Gossip	The Glory of God
Salvation of the Gentile	Laborers in the Vineyard
Assurance of Salvation	The Pearl of Great Price
A Thorn in the Flesh	The Angel Gabriel

CHAPTER THREE

The Textual Sermon

THE DEFINITION OF THE TEXTUAL SERMON

Textual and expository sermons are differentiated by two criteria: (1) How many verses of Scripture they use and (2) where their subdivisions and sub, subpoints come from. A textual sermon uses only one or two verses of Scripture from a biblical passage. In addition textual sermons derive their main divisions directly from the text but not the subdivisions nor any of their subpoints. When a text contains more than a few verses and yields the subdivisions (and any sub, subpoints) it is considered an expository sermon. Like topical sermons textual messages use the mechanical devices to create the remainder of the subdivisions. Making these distinctions is not so crucial because the idea of *Thematic Preaching* is that the sermon contents must be centered on the theme regardless of whether one crosses from preaching textually to expositorily.

Textual sermons are limited because they are dependent upon appropriate texts to preach from. A preacher can choose any one of the tens of thousands of verses in the Bible but not all those verses can be treated textually in the strictest sense of the word. An appropriate verse for a textual sermon must contain parallel ideas because if it doesn't then the preacher will be forced to use other methods to create the main divisions. Technically it will no longer be considered textual but probably a hybrid of more than one sermon type. In this case the preacher would be using one of the topical approaches or the expository method in order to create the main divisions.

We already touched on this earlier but our primary concern now is to explore the criteria of a good textual passage. As I stated an appropriate verse(s) to use for a textual message depends upon whether or not it contains parallel ideas.

EXAMPLES OF TEXTUAL OUTLINES

Example: Isa. 40:31

But they that wait upon the LORD shall renew their strength; they shall mount up with wings as eagles; they shall run, and not be weary; and they shall walk, and not faint.

Theme   *The Benefits of Waiting Upon the Lord*
Main Divisions:

    I. One benefit is renewed strength
    II. Another benefit is that they mount up with wings as eagles
    III. A third benefit is that when they run they will not grow weary
    IV. A fourth benefit is that when they walk they will not faint

Although some of these benefits are stated poetically and are a little redundant the point is clear. They are enumerated and stating them as main divisions is easy. Let's look at another verse we used earlier.

Example: Psalm 63:1

O God, thou art my God; early will I seek thee: my soul thirsteth for thee, my flesh longeth for thee in a dry and thirsty land, where no water is.

Theme   The Psalmist's Cry for the Presence of the Lord
Main Divisions:

I. The psalmist seeks the Lord
II. The psalmist thirsts for the Lord
III. The psalmist longs for the Lord

Example: John 3:18

He that believeth on him is not condemned: but he that believeth not is condemned already, because he hath not believed in the name of the only begotten Son of God.

Theme   The Absolute Necessity of Believing in Jesus
Main Divisions:

I. If you believe in Him you will not be condemned
II. If you do not believe in Him you will be condemned

Example: Ephesians 2:3

Among whom also we all had our conversation in times past in the lusts of our flesh, fulfilling the desires of the flesh and of the mind; and were by nature the children of wrath, even as others.

Theme   Our Former Lost Condition
Main Divisions:

I. We lusted in the flesh
II. We fulfilled the desires of our flesh and mind
III. We were by nature the children of wrath

Example: Eph. 4:31-32

Let all bitterness, and wrath, and anger, and clamour, and evil speaking, be put away from you, with all malice: And be ye kind one to another, tenderhearted, forgiving one another, even as God for Christ's sake hath forgiven you.

Theme   The Do's and Don'ts of Being a Loving
                 Christian
Main Divisions:

I. The Don'ts

      1. Don't be bitter
      2. Don't be wrathful
      3. Don't be angry
      4. Don't be clamorous
      5. Don't be slanderous
      6. Don't be malicious

II. The Do's
      1. Do be kind
      2. Do be tenderhearted
      3. Do be forgiving

Example: Eph. 3:20

Now unto him that is able to do exceeding abundantly above all that we ask or think, according to the power that worketh in us

Theme   The Exceeding Abundance of What God is Able to Do

Main Divisions:

  I. God is able to do exceedingly abundantly above all that we ask

  II. God is able to do exceedingly abundantly above all that we think

Example: Eph. 3:20-21

Now unto him that is able to do exceeding abundantly above all that we ask or think, according to the power that worketh in us, unto him be glory in the church by Christ Jesus throughout all ages, world without end. Amen.

Theme   A Benediction to God Almighty

Main Divisions:

  I. His Ability

      1. He can do exceedingly abundantly above all that we ask

2. He can do exceedingly abundantly above all that we think
II. His Agency: *According to the power that worketh in us*
III. His Accolades: *Be glory by Jesus Christ*
   1. In the church
   2. Throughout all ages
   3. World without end

This example is actually a combination between textual and expository. The number of verses makes it textual but the manner of treatment is expository. I included it here to show you that outlining both verse 20 and 21 of Ephesians 3 is not possible using the textual method alone. Originally I wanted to include verse 21 in the textual format but in order to complete the outline I had to resort to the expository method.

Notice main division number II in the example above. There are no subpoints but instead there is one, "equal" parallel thought separated by a colon. When the key noun of a main division has only one descriptive statement it should not be classified as a subpoint but rather as a thought of equal value. It should not, therefore, be used as a subpoint in the outline. From a literary standpoint it is not subordinate to the key noun (*agency*) but rather it clarifies or restates that noun more accurately. The same principle applies to main division number III above.

Example: 2 Corinthians 7:1

Having therefore these promises, dearly beloved, let us cleanse ourselves from all filthiness of the flesh and spirit, perfecting holiness in the fear of God.

Theme   Living Righteously in the Light of the
             Promises of God
Main Divisions:

   I. We live righteously by cleansing ourselves from all filthiness of the flesh and spirit
  II. We live righteously by perfecting holiness in the fear of God

Notice that the key element of the theme is *living righteously* rather than the *promises of God.* Naturally, they are related because we live righteously on account of the promises of God. Living righteously, therefore, is what should be developed in the main divisions. There is a degree of flexibility if you feel led to stress something else in the verse. If you want to place the primary emphasis on the *promises of God* we can restate the divisions this way:

   I. *The promises of God* motivate us to cleanse ourselves from all filthiness of the flesh and spirit
  II. *The promises of God* motivate us to perfect holiness in the fear of God

In either case when you preach this message you will, no doubt, lay sufficient emphasis on both aspects. You cannot help but to do so because it is integral to your main divisions. The point is that you have flexibility to state the divisions in a manner that does justice to the main idea as well as the freedom necessary to stress what you feel the Lord is leading you to preach.

Example: 1 Thessalonians 1:5

For our gospel came not unto you in word only, but also in power, and in the Holy Ghost, and in much assurance; as ye know what manner of men we were among you for your sake.

Theme   How the Gospel of Christ Came to the
             Thessalonians
Main Divisions:

I.   The Gospel of Christ came in power
II. The Gospel of Christ came in the Holy Ghost
III. The Gospel of Christ came in much assurance

Example: 1 Thessalonians 5:23

And the very God of peace sanctify you wholly; and I pray God your whole spirit and soul and body be preserved blameless unto the coming of our Lord Jesus Christ.

Theme   A Benediction for Total Sanctification
Main Divisions:

I.   A desired blessing that their whole spirit would be preserved blameless unto the 2nd coming of Christ
II. A desired blessing that their soul would be preserved blameless unto the 2nd coming of Christ
III. A desired blessing that their body be preserved blameless unto the 2nd coming of Christ

Example: 1 Cor. 13:13

And now abideth faith, hope, charity, these three; but the greatest of these is charity.

Theme   Love: The greatest of the three eternal
             virtues
Main Divisions:

I.   Love is greater than faith
II. Love is greater than hope

Alternate Theme   The Three Great Eternal Virtues
Main Divisions:

   I.   What they are
       1. Faith
       2. Hope
       3. Love
   II.   How they compare
       1. Love is greater than faith
       2. Love is greater than hope

This alternate outline is another example of a hybrid between the textual and expository methods. It is textual because only a few verses are involved but it is expository due to its manner of treatment. In this case the textual method does not yield the fullness that the expository method does.

Example: Romans 9:4

Who are Israelites; to whom pertaineth the adoption, and the glory, and the covenants, and the giving of the law, and the service of God, and the promises

Theme   The Prerogatives of Israelites
Main Divisions:

   I.   To the Israelites pertains the right of adoption
   II. To the Israelites pertains the right of glory
   III. To the Israelites pertains the right of the covenants
   IV. To the Israelites pertains the right of the giving of the law
   V. To the Israelites pertains the right of the service of God
   VI. To the Israelites pertains the right of the promises

Example: 1 Tim. 1:17

Now unto the King eternal, immortal, invisible, the only wise God, be honour and glory for ever and ever. Amen.

Theme   The Characteristics of the King
Main Divisions:

    I.   The King is immortal
    II.   The King is invisible
    III.   The King is wise

Alternate Theme   A Benediction for the King
Main Divisions:

  I.   His attributes
      1) The King is immortal
      2) The King is invisible
      3) The King is wise
  II.   His accolades
      1) Unto the King be honor forever
      2) Unto the King be glory forever

This is the third example of combining the textual method with the expository. In each case the textual method was insufficient to do justice to the content of the verses. We needed to use exposition. Does it matter whether or not you cross the line? Of course not. You, however, should be aware of the possibilities available to you.

Notice that in the first example of 1 Timothy 1:17 I essentially used the "characteristics of" approach that we learned in the topical message plan. This particular sermon plan is not topical, however, because the main divisions come directly from the text. What this demonstrates is that the biblical writers used the same manner of logical organization that characterizes our topical sermon approaches. It is the way they wrote. Expressing yourself with parallel ideas makes sense. Thus *Thematic Preaching* has its foundation based in practicality, literary unity, and logic.

In the example of 1 Corinthians 13:13 the alternate theme may seem redundant but each case has a slightly different emphasis. In actuality I prefer the second choice for the simple reason that before you begin to exalt love above faith and hope you must know what all three mean. The verse is not just a comparison between love and the others. It is a declaration that all three are important. Your sermon plan should reflect this.

THE DO'S AND DON'TS OF THE TEXTUAL SERMON

Now that we have viewed numerous examples of textual sermons there are some pointers that the reader should keep in mind before deciding upon a particular text to preach. Keep in mind that some of the following admonitions apply to the other sermon types as well.

1. Choose the right text for the right occasion. If you are delivering a message at a wedding choose a hopeful, positive, and practical text that will encourage the bride and groom. Why would you choose something that is morbid and depressing?

2. Avoid texts whose themes are too broad to cover in one sermon. We stated in the earlier chapters that broad themes tend to yield sermons that are shallow and lack purpose. You cannot do justice to the whole counsel of God in one sermon. Avoid texts that yield such broad themes and subject matter.

3. Avoid using a text as means of jesting with the audience. A little bit of humor is OK and may even be desirable at times. For example, "Did you know Joshua had no parents?" "It says he was the son of Nun!" No one should be offended by this quip but sometimes preachers take liberties and go too far with the word of God. They jest about inappropriate subject matter using the Scriptures to do so. Avoid offending both God and the spiritually-minded people in your audience who will take exception to your irreverent sense of humor.

4. Avoid using a fragment of a verse for a text. Occasionally you might get away with producing a good sermon using a fragment but it is best to use the entire verse rather than plucking a phrase out of it to preach from. It violates a principle of *Thematic Preaching* that emphasizes the natural literary flow to develop your sermon around. You cannot extrapolate a theme when there isn't one. A two-word fragment does not contain a theme. By the way, the shortest verse in the Bible, "*Jesus wept "(Jn. 11:35)*, is not a fragment. It is a complete sentence containing subject and predicate.

5. If you want to preach strictly textual sermons you must choose texts that contain parallel ideas. If you choose a text that does not contain them you will be doing more work and crossing over into the other sermon types. If you don't mind then by all means do so.

6. Do not choose texts that are spurious. If the textual grounds of a verse are highly questionable why

choose it to preach from? The preacher of the English Bible cannot afford to be distracted with the minority vs. majority text debate but there are many verses in Scripture that both schools of thought regard as spurious. Avoid those texts because they are probably not, in fact, the Word of God.

7. Do not choose texts that record the sayings of uninspired men and women. If you choose a verse or passage spoken by one of Job's three friends you are using a text spoken by a flawed person. You might be making the same mistake that they did. All Scripture is equally inspired but all Scripture is not equally relevant.

8. Be sure to choose texts that offer variety to your congregation. Do not get hung up on biblical passages that always emphasize the same truth. Someone once said that if a person is always mentioning the same thing then to him it is a problem.

9. Never choose a text that is aimed at attacking someone in the audience. The pulpit is a holy place not to be defiled by sinful human jealousy and anger. If you have problems with someone in the pew then go to him privately and settle the issue.

10. Do not choose a text that is overly complex or obscure. Language translation, textual criticism, lack of historical data, etc. are all reasons why the meaning of a verse has remained uncertain. A sermon can only be as authoritative as our understanding of the word.

CHAPTER FOUR

An Introduction to the Expository Sermon

THE DEFINITION OF BIBLICAL EXPOSITION

An expository sermon uses three or more verses of Scripture whose main points, subpoints, and sub, subpoints come directly from the text whether repeated verbatim or replaced with dynamic equivalents. In addition expository sermons differ from textual sermons in their manner of treatment. Textual sermons use parallel statements relating to the same theme in order to create the main divisions. The subpoints typically come from one of the topical approaches. Expository sermons, on the other hand, essentially use the "aspects of" approach (within the confines of the text that is) in order to create the main divisions. In addition all subpoints come from the text as well. Unlike the topical sermon plan, however, both the theme and all divisions come directly from the passage and not from the preacher's own knowledge of the subject.

THE STRENGTHS AND WEAKNESS OF EXPOSITION

Biblical exposition is the best overall method of preaching for several reasons.

1) It offers variety to listeners. Unless a preacher goes out of his way to find passages containing the same subject matter week after week listeners will hear different parts of the Bible every Sunday. Preaching expositorily encourages the predication of the whole counsel of God.

2) It is the best method for clearly portraying the original meaning of the text. Expository sermons

trace the themes of Scripture thereby accurately reflecting the author's original intentions for writing. Preaching the Scriptures contextually is the most faithful manner of delivering the Word of God.

3) It is without question the most authoritative method of sermon delivery. The nature of expository sermons is to find the themes present in Scripture and preach them. In other words, exposition attempts to preach what the writers of Scripture have already proclaimed. The authority of the Word of God remains central, not one man's ability or knowledge.

4) The expositor does not have to struggle finding subject matter to preach. If he is preaching through a Bible book the Holy Spirit has already inspired the sermon material.

5) Once biblical exposition is mastered creating outlines from passages is a very time-efficient method of sermon preparation. Compared to other methods biblical exposition can save the preacher valuable time in the study.

6) It is the most comprehensive and practical method of preparing sermons. Textual sermons are more restrictive than exposition. Topical messages, on the other hand, depend on the preacher's ability to think up new material to preach.

Biblical exposition has its weaknesses as well. The weaknesses usually lie with the expositor and not with the method itself.

1) Biblical exposition takes a lot of hard work and discipline to perfect. It is a unique art form of the English language (or whatever language is used) as much as it is a science of sermon preparation. Unless a preacher is willing to pay the price that patience demands and persist in spite of the many mistakes he will make along the way he will never master the art. It is too easy to get discouraged because of the amount of discipline and brain twisting, mental exercise required.

2) Unless care is taken an expository sermon can be reduced to a running monologue of the text. The audience can read for itself and does not need a preacher simply repeating what the Bible already says. Preachers who pride themselves on the fact that they preach expositorily may be in for a surprise to know that their congregations have grown weary of their monotonous, running commentaries on the Bible. When I began preaching in my church a member of my congregation expressed concern to me because up to that point all the expository messages he had heard were nothing more than monotonous monologues of the obvious. He was not impressed with the authority factor. If this was the case why should he be? The sermons he had heard did not possess purpose. I hope I convinced him otherwise.

3) In addition to the previous point every sermon must have purpose as well as what I termed earlier, "the punch factor." It is easy for expositors to forget this. He must make sure he is driving a specific spiritual lesson home. He needs to make

the necessary practical applications to ensure he is feeding his people. An expository sermon that lacks the punch factor can be equated to a person who eats plenty of food but is dying of malnutrition because of a lack of essential nutrients.

4) Because biblical exposition requires the use of whole passages it is very easy to cover too much information. It takes flexibility and wisdom to limit that information that an expositor would otherwise overload the audience with.

5) The advantage of always having material to preach can also be a disadvantage. Preachers can get lazy and forgetful of the fact that the Holy Spirit is still in charge and ultimately is the one who spiritually energizes a sermon. Expositors can become stubborn and may resist the Spirit's promptings to move in another direction when led to. We must never forget that the Lord does not use His Word without prayer and the Spirit's guidance.

THE METHODOLOGY OF BIBLICAL EXPOSITION

In chapter three I gave you an overview of the three major sermon types in an attempt to introduce you to fact that each sermon type utilized a theme in order to create the main divisions. I used Rev. 2:1-7 *The Message to the Church at Ephesus* as the theme. I will now use a related passage, Rev. 3:1-6, *The Message to the Church at Sardis* as the theme.

Example: Rev. 3:1-6

And unto the angel of the church in Sardis write; These things saith he that hath the seven Spirits of God, and the seven stars; I know thy works, that thou hast a name that thou livest, and art dead.

2 Be watchful, and strengthen the things which remain, that are ready to die: for I have not found thy works perfect before God. 3 Remember therefore how thou hast received and heard, and hold fast, and repent. If therefore thou shalt not watch, I will come on thee as a thief, and thou shalt not know what hour I will come upon thee. 4 Thou hast a few names even in Sardis which have not defiled their garments; and they shall walk with me in white: for they are worthy. 5 He that overcometh, the same shall be clothed in white raiment; and I will not blot out his name out of the book of life, but I will confess his name before my Father, and before his angels. 6 He that hath an ear, let him hear what the Spirit saith unto the churches.

Theme   The Message to the Church of Sardis
Sermon Type   Exposition
Main Divisions:

1. The Captain of the Church (1a)
2. The Correction to the Church (1b)
3. The Command to the Church (2-3)
4. The Commendation of the Church (4)
5. The Commitment to the Church (5)
6. The Counsel to the Church (6)

While this outline is slightly different than the example of the Ephesian Church in chapter 3 the similarities are obvious. Each letter to the seven churches uses the same format. Each of these main divisions is an aspect of the theme *The Message to the Church at Sardis.* One aspect of this letter is the Captain of the Church (*These things saith he that hath the seven Spirits of God, and the seven stars).* A second aspect is the rebuke or the correction to the Church (*I know thy works, that thou hast a name that thou livest, and art dead).* A third aspect is the command to the Church (*be watchful, strengthen, repent),* etc. The passage of Scripture is broken down accordingly. While there are some variations to the expository method as a whole there is a common thread in *Thematic Preaching* noticeable in every possible scenario of outlining a sermon.

Example: Romans 8:18-23

18For I reckon that the sufferings of this present time are not worthy to be compared with the glory which shall be revealed in us. 19For the earnest expectation of the creature waiteth for the manifestation of the sons of God. 20For the creature was made subject to vanity, not willingly, but by reason of him who hath subjected the same in hope, 21Because the creature itself also shall be delivered from the bondage of corruption into the glorious liberty of the children of God. 22 For we know that the whole creation groans and labors with birth pangs together until now. 23 Not only that, but we also who have the firstfruits of the Spirit, even we ourselves groan within ourselves, eagerly waiting for the adoption, the redemption of our body.

Theme   The suffering involved in waiting for our glorification (taken from vs.18)

Main Divisions:

    I.   The Perspective of Suffering (18) *i.e. put into perspective suffering is worth it*

    II.   The Patience in Suffering (19) *i.e. the suffering is an anxious waiting game for our glorification*

    III.   The Provenance of Suffering (20) *i.e. The source. It is God who subjected us to this vanity and it is God who also subjected us to the eternal hope (the implication is that God put the feeling of vanity in us to cause us to hope for the eternal)*

    IV.   The Postponement of our Suffering (21) *i.e. one day we shall all be changed from the bondage of corruption into glorified saints of God and suffering will end.*

    V.   The Prevalence of Suffering (22-23)

        1. The prevalence in the whole world (22)

        2. The prevalence in believers (23)

Examine each of these main divisions and see if you agree whether or not they represent the truth presented in the verses. These divisions did not come easy. The theme is found in verse 18 and the rest of the text relates to it. The difficulty of this example is zoning in on the right theme. When I began working on it I was making the mistake of emphasizing *our future glorious change* as the central motif rather than the suffering involved in waiting for it. My theme was *Our future glorious hope amid suffering*. When I tried to pull the main divisions from verses 19-23 I could not understand why they wouldn't come together. The reason is because these verses deal more with the suffering involved in waiting for our glorious change rather than the glorious change itself. In other words the motif of pain is primary while the motif of our glorious change is secondary. Yes, because it is so glorious we suffer all the more.

Because my theme was wrong I could not create the main divisions. Something was wrong. When you have chosen a wrong theme you will find yourself forcing the divisions to make sense. This should send up a red flag that you are using the wrong theme. Once I realized my mistake, however, I changed the theme to *The Suffering Involved in Waiting for our Future Glorious Hope* and the divisions immediately coalesced. The aspect of suffering is the primary motif which the rest of the text verifies. This mental exercise is common to *Thematic Preaching* so the reader should be prepared to do a lot of it.

The textual method requires the preacher to find parallel ideas and creates the main divisions out of them. Unfortunately there are no such parallel ideas here and therefore even if you wanted to use the textual method it would not be possible. You must use the "aspects of" approach to create these divisions. Like the textual method the main divisions in the expository sermon come directly from the text (either the exact words or a dynamic equivalent). If you choose a few verses and there are no parallel thoughts then you treat it expositorily or topically, whichever seems to be the best method. If there are parallel ideas then it makes sense to treat it textually. Parallelism is a key factor, however, in all methods of sermon preparation.

Example: 1 Cor. 5:1-8

It is reported commonly that there is fornication among you, and such fornication as is not so much as named among the Gentiles, that one should have his father's wife. 2 And ye are puffed up, and have not rather mourned, that he that hath done this deed might be taken away from among you. 3 For I verily, as absent in body, but present in spirit, have judged already, as though I were present, concerning him that hath so done this deed, 4 In the name of our Lord Jesus Christ, when ye are gathered together, and my spirit, with the power of our Lord Jesus Christ, 5 To deliver such an one unto Satan for the destruction of the flesh, that the spirit may be saved in the day of the Lord Jesus. 6 Your glorying is not good. Know ye not that a little leaven leaveneth the whole lump? 7 Purge out therefore the old leaven, that ye may be a new lump, as ye are unleavened. For even Christ our passover is sacrificed for us: 8 Therefore let us keep the feast, not with old leaven, neither with the leaven of malice and wickedness; but with the unleavened bread of sincerity and truth.

Theme   The Sin of Immorality in the Church
Type   Biblical Exposition
Main Divisions:

    I.   The Repulsiveness of their sin (1)   *"that one should have his father's wife"*

II.   The Rebuke for their sin (2) *"And ye are puffed up"*

III.   The Retribution for their sin (3-5)
1.   The Source of that retribution (3) *"I . . . have judged already"*
2.   The Solidarity of that retribution (4) *"when ye are gathered together"*
3.   The Severity of that retribution (5) *"To deliver such an one unto Satan for the destruction of the flesh"*

IV.   The Recommendation for their sin (6-8)
1.   Recommended to stop glorying (6) *"Your glorying is not good"*
2.   Recommended to purge out the old leaven (7) *"Purge out therefore the old leaven"*
3.   Recommended to keep the feast (8) *"let us keep the feast"*

The above three examples demonstrate the practicality of organizing your sermon around the theme. The divisions logically follow the author's train of thought. The main divisions reflect the change in each thought. Keep in mind that choosing the right theme depends upon the expositor's ability to zone in on the main noun in the theme. In the first example, Rev. 3:1-6, the key noun is *message*. All the main divisions stress an aspect of this message. In the second example, Rom. 8:18-23, the key noun is *suffering*. The central idea of each main division deals with suffering. In the third example, 1 Cor. 5:1-8, the key noun is *sin* or *immorality*. All the main divisions stress some aspect of their sin of immorality. *Preaching Thematically* means you must ascertain the right theme in order for your divisions to fall into place.

THE USE OF ALLITERATION IN EXPOSITORY SERMONS

Its Purpose

If you have followed my sermon outlines in the previous examples you have noticed that they are usually alliterated. To alliterate is to use the same letter of the alphabet for the key noun in each main division. For example: The *repulsiveness*, the *rebuke*, the *retribution*, and the *recommendation* for the Corinthians' sin of immorality. You can also alliterate (for lack of a better term) by virtue of sound and style. For example, *commission, obsession, regression*, and *contrition*. All of these words possess a similar sound and benefit the preacher and listeners. There are good reasons to use alliteration. It is not just to be cute or poetic in order to impress the audience. Alliteration aids the preacher in the following ways:

1. It encourages simplicity. Remember one of the rules of thumb for stating a good theme that we mentioned in chapter two? *Simplicity.* The theme should be as simple as possible (even though it will be difficult at times). Likewise, alliteration encourages the main divisions of an outline to be stated simply as well. It tends to restrict lengthy and awkward statements to a more easily understandable sentence or phrase.

2. It serves as a memory aid both for the preacher and the audience. When the main divisions are alliterated the preacher has an easier time remembering them. The retrieval of information from the memory banks of the brain is a challenge to a preacher who has a lot on his mind.

Alliteration makes it easier to recall that information. In addition it also benefits the audience by making it easy for them to remember those concise points.

3. It tends to promote divisions that are parallel with one another. Choosing alliterative words means that you have already attempted to correlate the subject matter in a logical fashion. It means you have compared the thoughts with one another and have attempted to organize them so that the audience can understand more easily.

4. While the first three reasons are enough to warrant alliteration the fourth reason is the greatest: It forces the expositor to explore the many possible applications available in each main division. For example, if you have the theme *The Rapture of the Church* the main divisions for that theme could be the *time* of the rapture, the *occasion* for the rapture and the *seriousness* of the rapture. As you attempt to find synonyms for each of these divisions all beginning with the same first letter you may come across more pertinent aspects than the ones you first thought of. Your search will yield synonyms that are more descriptive than the original and it will also reveal other main divisions that you will want to include. By searching for a synonym you have opened up the possibilities available for that main division as well as for other potential main divisions. The use of alliteration, therefore, aids both with the interpretation and application of the text.

5. The search for appropriate synonyms can be mentally taxing as well as time consuming. The fringe benefit of overcoming these two obstacles, however, is that the expositor inadvertently makes himself thoroughly familiar with his text. He will know his material inside and out.

Its Pit Falls

1. Attempting to be cute rather than accurate. Alliteration is a beneficial tool for the expositor as the reasons above make abundantly clear. Unfortunately good things are always abused and because of the abuse some refuse to use alliteration because they do not want to be identified with the guilty. Alliteration is a means to an end, not an end in itself. Its purpose is to clarify the main divisions for both the audience and the speaker. When used carelessly, however, it annoys listeners who cannot make the connections between the main divisions in spite of the brilliant poetry. People in the audience will conclude that part of the problem with the preacher's incoherent message is his attempt to be cute instead of being accurate. Alliteration must never take the place of accuracy and precision.

2. Obscuring the meaning rather than aiding it. Alliteration opens up the range of possibilities for each division but it can obscure the meaning instead if the expositor is not careful. For example, if I am attempting to find a synonym for "declaration" that starts with 'p' I find the following possibilities in a thesaurus: *pitch, presentation,*

profession, promulgation, profession, protestation, and publication. Depending upon the context in which "declaration" is being used some of these synonyms will be more accurate than others. *Presentation* might describe "declaration" more precisely than *publication.* Just because it is a synonym listed in the thesaurus does not mean it accurately matches the nuance of that word in that particular context. Words have shades of meaning and nuances and only the context will determine if an expositor is using a word wisely. Preachers can be careless and the audience will quickly realize when the preacher sacrifices accuracy for the sake of alliteration.

3. Another problem with alliteration is that often an expositor may feel his message is both organized and coherent solely on the basis of alliteration. Consider the following example when Jesus calmed the storm:

Matt. 8:23-27

The Ship
The Storm
The Spirit
The Scared
The Savior
The Surprise

Is this a good sermon outline? What logically connects these divisions with one another? What is the theme? The theme of a sermon acts like glue ensuring that the main divisions all relate to it and to one another. Nothing in this sermon plan does this. If the sermon does not have a good theme the main divisions will be disjointed and unrelated to the rest of the sermon. The preacher is at risk of giving six mini sermons.

These divisions need a unifying theme in order for them to make sense. If the theme is somewhat vague (as themes in historical narrative can be) then the preacher needs a subtheme or title expressing the spiritual direction the sermon will take. Without the proper theme this sermon is nothing more than individual statements that probably won't relate to one another.

CHAPTER FIVE

Hybrid Sermon Types

THE TEXTUAL EXPOSITORY SERMON

I have included this sermon type here because it falls under the category of the textual sermon even though it is very unique. It is textual because the main divisions come directly from the verses of Scripture yet it is also expository because you must use at least four verses. Dr. John Benson described this sermon type as *a sermon in which the main divisions derive from parallel expressions in several non-consecutive verses of Scripture.*[13] The idea is to find parallel expressions that are located in different portions of Scripture and create the main divisions out of them. You need at least four different verses that are not consecutive whose ideas are parallel. You must use the exact words of the text. You cannot use an alternate or equivalent meaning of a word or phrase in place of the original. You must use the exact parallelism found in the Bible. More often than not you will be looking for a key word or phrase that you can find others to match. The use of a concordance is very helpful. Below is an example with instructions how to create a textual expository sermon out of the selected verses.

Example:

Key Words   "God is"
Parallel Phrases:

God is jealous	Deuteronomy 6:15
God is gracious	2 Chronicles 30:9

---

[13]Benson, 79.

God is wise	Job 9:4
God is holy	Psalm 99:9
God is merciful	Psalm 116:5
God is righteous	Daniel 9:14
God is true	John 3:33
God is Spirit	John 4:24
God is faithful	1 Corinthians 1:9
God is one	Galatians 3:20
God is light	1 John 1:5
God is love	1 John 4:8

1. Choose a phrase that you think is 'preachable.' For this example we will use "God is."
2. Look up the references in a concordance and list them. Needless to say it will yield many phrases of which the above is only a portion.
3. Choose a theme that unites some of them together based on parallel ideas and form. These will be used as the main divisions of the sermon body. This step is crucial in creating an outline that is truly parallel. For example, one of these phrases is "God is my King." While this statement is parallel in form with the others it is not parallel in thought. The choice of your theme will dictate which phrases should remain and which should be eliminated. You can see that the statements above speak of God's attributes. In fact, that is the only theme possible for this example. Our theme for this example, therefore, is *The Attributes of God.* "God is my judge" does not state an attribute but what He does for us or what He is to us. We could change it to "God is just" but then it would not be

original. We must not alter the original words of the text at all.

4. Eliminate any phrases that are not parallel with the rest. Viewing above you can see that there are two that are slightly different than the others. "God is spirit" (John 4:24) and "God is one" (Galatians 3:20) are not quite the same as the others. Indeed they are attributes but differ with respect to the kind of attribute they are. "God is spirit" and "God is one" speak of God's basic constituency. Spirit and oneness are amoral attributes of God. We are flesh and bone but He is spirit. The rest, however, are moral attributes. You may choose not to be as picky when you prepare your sermon but I prefer to keep things completely parallel because listeners appreciate coherence.

Example:

Key words: "God is"
Theme   Who God is to me
Parallel Phrases and Main Divisions:

1. God is My Portion   Psalm 73:26
2. God is My King   Psalm 74:12
3. God is My Witness   Philippians 1:8
4. God is My Salvation   Isaiah 12:2
5. God is My Power   2 Samuel 22:33
6. God is My Helper   Psalm 54:4
7. God is My Defense   Psalm 59:9
8. God is My Strength   Habakkuk 3:19

Example:

Key words   "of the cross"
Theme   The Cross of Christ
Main Divisions:

I.	The Preaching of the Cross	1 Cor. 1:18
II.	The Offense of the Cross	Galatians 5:11
III.	The Death of the Cross	Philippians 2:8
IV.	The Enemies of the Cross	Phil. 3:18

There are many other phrases that contain the word "cross" in it such as "endured the cross" (Heb. 12:2), "persecution for the cross" (Gal. 6:12), "come down from the cross" (Mk. 15:30), etc. but they are not parallel with the others. *Thematic Preaching* is biblical preaching because it emphasizes tracing the themes of Scripture, even in this case. Admittedly this technique is a little unique but it still emphasizes the themes of Scripture. This method does not use one particular passage as the other types but, nevertheless, has its authority based in the Word of God.

Example:

Key words   "one another"
Theme   Exhortations Concerning One Another
Main Divisions:

I.	Love One Another	John 13:34
II.	Prefer One Another	Rom. 12:10
III.	Receive One Another	Rom. 15:7
IV.	Admonish one Another	Rom. 15:14
V.	Greet One Another	1 Cor. 16:20
VI.	Serve One Another	Gal. 5:13

VII.	Forbear One Another	Eph. 4:2
VIII.	Forgive One Another	Eph. 4:32
IX.	Comfort One Another	1 Thess. 4:18
X.	Edify One Another	1 Thess. 5:11
XI.	Exhort One Another	Heb. 3:13
XII.	Consider One Another	Heb. 10:24

Again, there are other 'one another' phrases that do not fit this exact form yet contain similar truth. While there is nothing spiritually wrong using them we like to keep our thoughts parallel in every respect in order to create good habits when *Preaching Thematically.* Likewise some of the other phrases fit the form but do not belong for obvious reasons. For example, Titus 3:3 "hating one another" and Rev. 6:4 "kill one another." These statements are parallel in form but not in thought. The 'one another' phrases above are all positive things, not negative.

Example:

Key words   "I am"
Verses:

John 6:35	I am the bread of life
John 8:12	I am the light of the world
John 10:7	I am the door
John 10:11	I am the good shepherd
John 11:25	I am the resurrection and the life
John 14:6	I am the way, the truth, and the life
John 15:5	I am the vine

Theme   Who Jesus said He is
Main Divisions:

   I.   I Am the Bread of Life (6:35)
   II.   I Am the Light of the World (8:12)

III.   I Am the Door (10:7)
IV.   I Am the Good Shepherd (10:11)
V.   I Am the Resurrection and the Life (11:25)
VI.   I Am the Way, the Truth, and the Life (14:6)
VII.   I Am the Vine (15:5)

Jesus also said "I am not of this world" (John 17:14) but this does not fit the format above. There is no question that you could preach about the fact that Jesus is not of this world but this would cause discontinuity in our outline. Yes, indeed, you might not care and preach it anyway. That is not the point, however. We are trying to discipline your mind so that when you are *Preaching Thematically* you will naturally organize your thoughts logically. If you don't care and state your divisions haphazardly eventually it will come back to bite you. Someone in your congregation is bound to let you know about your lack of coherence.

THE TOPICAL TEXTUAL SERMON: The Inferential Sermon

The diversity of ten topical approaches, the expository and textual methods, and the textual-expository method will take you very far in your sermon preparation skills. You have sufficient knowledge to deliver biblically sound, logical, and coherent messages that will inspire your congregation. There is a hybrid type that will be beneficial to add to your repertoire of sermon methods. It is called the topical-textual method. Like the textual-expository sermon this also is unique.

All of the previous methods attempt to state exactly what the text is saying even if you use dynamic equivalents in place of the original words of Scripture. The main divisions state precisely what is found in the Word of God. With this method, however, the preacher draws inferences that the text implies. It is an interpretive method of creating main points for your sermon body. The task is not to state what the text clearly says, but what it implies.

Example: Rom. 8:18-21

18 For I consider that the sufferings of this present time are not worthy to be compared with the glory which shall be revealed in us. 19 For the earnest expectation of the creation eagerly waits for the revealing of the sons of God. 20 For the creation was subjected to futility, not willingly, but because of Him who subjected it in hope; 21 because the creation itself also will be delivered from the bondage of corruption into the glorious liberty of the children of God. (NKJV)

1. Find a biblical passage that contains many truths that you can identify. These truths are inferences and not the obvious meaning of the verse. We will demonstrate using a previous example.
2. Find the right theme. We already decided that the correct one for this passage is *The suffering involved in waiting for our future glorious hope.* As I will discuss in more detail some genres of biblical literature allow more flexibility when choosing the right theme. In other words when you extract your implications you may decide to alter the theme somewhat in order for them to work. This is not the case for Romans 8:18-21. This passage does not permit any alterations. Below you will see other examples where you can justifiably alter your theme to match your implications.
3. List all the ramifications or deductions that are implied in the passage. Remember not to state what the text already says. If you do you are not drawing inferences from the text. If you don't want

to draw inferences you can always rely on the other methods to prepare your sermon. There is no point to this method if it does not accomplish something unique.

4. Work with each implication until you are sure it makes sense. You may have to adjust your wording as you attempt to relate it to your theme.

Here is the list of truths:

1. Christians cannot avoid suffering *"the suffering of this present life"*
   --implies inevitability
2. Christians should put suffering into perspective *"are not worthy to be compared"*
   -- implies longing for something better
3. This suffering consists of an anxious waiting game for our glorification in heaven *"the earnest expectation of the creation waits"*
   --implies that waiting for our glorification is not easy even though it is greatly desired
4. God subjected us to this suffering in order that we might long for eternity *"For the creature was made subject to vanity, not willingly but by reason of him"*
   – implies God's ultimate purpose is to cause us to hope for the eternal
5. Christians have no choice but to face suffering as part of God's plan for maturity *"not willingly"*
   -- Implies God's sovereignty over the affairs of men
6. Our future glorification highlights our present bondage all the more *"the bondage of corruption"*
   —implies all humans, saved and lost, feel the futility of this sinful life in comparison to heaven
7. Longing for our perfect, future liberty increases our suffering now (while increasing our hope also) *"into the glorious liberty of the children of God"*

-- implies that we are not completely at liberty now by comparison

Each number above contains three things: (1) The overall implication you will use as your main division. (2) The portion of Scripture that leads you to make that deduction. (3) A rationale for the basis for your implication. I added this third factor simply to help you understand the thought process. You do not need to add this to your sermon preparation plan. I included it here for explanation's sake only.

Notice that all of these divisions closely correlate to the theme. Furthermore, all contain the key word "suffering" and all relate that suffering to the waiting game of our glorification. Some of the implications are more readily seen than others but all relate in some manner. If they don't then you must remove them because they will take you on a tangent away from your theme. Notice also that all the implications are complete sentences. Do not use phrases as your main divisions. This sermon type is unique in this respect. Thus, our sermon plan would look like this:

Theme   The suffering involved with waiting for our future glorious hope
Sermon Type   Topical Textual
Text   Rom. 8:18-21
Main Divisions:

    I.   Christians cannot avoid suffering (18a)
    II.   Christians should put suffering into perspective (18)
    III.   Suffering is an anxious waiting game for our glorification in heaven (19)

IV. God subjected us to suffering so that we might long for eternity (20a)

V. Christians must face suffering as part of God's plan for maturity (20b)

VI. Future glorification highlights our present bondage all the more (21a)

VII. Longing for our future liberty increases our suffering now (21b)

Another important thing to consider is that your audience should not struggle when they listen to your implications. Admittedly the above example is a tough one. There are many portions of Scripture that are much easier to make the obvious, logical deductions. If listeners seem clueless it may be because you are stretching when you draw your inferences. Scripture does not need your help! The inferences should be as obvious and natural as possible. You must discipline yourself to say only what the text implies.

Example: 1 Cor. 5:1-5

1 It is actually reported that there is sexual immorality among you, and such sexual immorality as is not even named among the Gentiles—that a man has his father's wife! 2 And you are puffed up, and have not rather mourned, that he who has done this deed might be taken away from among you. 3 For I indeed, as absent in body but present in spirit, have already judged (as though I were present) him who has so done this deed. 4 In the name of our Lord Jesus Christ, when you are gathered together, along with my spirit, with the power of our Lord Jesus Christ, 5 deliver such a one to Satan for the destruction of the flesh, that his spirit may be saved in the day of the Lord Jesus. (NKJV)

Following the steps above,

Example: 1 Cor. 5:1-5

The theme: Immorality In The Church
The inferences are as follows:

I. Fornication in the church is well known(1a)
   "It is reported commonly that there is fornication among you"

II. The sin of believers is often worse than the world (1b) *"as is not even named among the Gentiles"*

III. The sin of pride is present when there is open immorality (2a) *"And ye are puffed up, and have not rather mourned"*

IV. Deliberate separation from sinning believers pleases God (2b) *"that he who has done this deed might be taken away from among you"*

V. Serious sexual sin in the church affects even those who are far away (3a) *"I indeed, as absent in body but present in spirit"*

VI. The godly overseers of the church are endued with spiritual authority to deal with open sin (3b) *"have judged already, as though I were present"*

VII. Church discipline is a public, corporate effort (4) *"when you are gathered together, along with my spirit"*

VIII. The Lord uses Satan as a tool of chastisement for his sinning children (5a) *"deliver such a one to Satan"*

IX. The ultimate goal of church discipline is the saving of the soul from sin (5b) *"that his spirit may be saved in the day of the Lord Jesus"*

X. God is more concerned with your holiness than he is about your own life (5) *"for the destruction of the flesh, that the spirit may be saved in the day of the Lord Jesus"*

The final step is to reword these to ensure that they correspond to the theme. Each of these does. They all contain the primary idea of immorality or sin in the church.

Example: John 13:6-10

6 Then He came to Simon Peter. And Peter said to Him, "Lord, are You washing my feet?" 7 Jesus answered and said to him, "What I am doing you do not understand now, but you will know after this." 8 Peter said to Him, "You shall never wash my feet!" Jesus answered him, "If I do not wash you, you have no part with Me." 9 Simon Peter said to Him, "Lord, not my feet only, but also my hands and my head!" 10 Jesus said to him, "He who is bathed needs only to wash his feet, but is completely clean; and you are clean, but not all of you." (NKJV)

Theme: Jesus' gracious, humble ministry to his unconverted children

Inferences:

    I.   The Divine, humble service is not logical to the unconverted (6a) *"are You washing my feet?"*

    II.   Only converted people understand His ministry (7) *"but you will know after this"*

    III.   The unconverted naturally reject the gracious acts of God (8a) *"You shall never wash my feet"*

    IV.   Submission to His divine, humble act is absolutely necessary if conversion is going to take place (8b) *"If I do not wash you, you have no part with Me"*

    V.   The unconverted always want to add to His gracious work (9) *"Lord, not my feet only, but also my hands and my head!"*

    VI.   The Spirit's work of regeneration is the only sufficient means to convert the unconverted (10) *"He who is bathed needs only to wash his feet, but is completely clean"*

Check each of these and see if they align with the theme of the passage. You will see that they do.

Example: John 3:1-4

1 There was a man of the Pharisees, named Nicodemus, a ruler of the Jews: 2 The same came to Jesus by night, and said unto him, Rabbi, we know that thou art a teacher come from God: for no man can do these miracles that thou doest, except God be with him. 3 Jesus answered and said unto him, Verily, verily, I say unto thee, Except a man be born again, he cannot see the kingdom of God. 4 Nicodemus saith unto him, How can a man be born when he is old? can he enter the second time into his mother's womb, and be born?

Theme: The Conduct of Lost Religious Leaders
Inferences:

I.   They take pride in their status (1) *"a man of the Pharisees"* (implied)

II.   Their shame is a testimony to their lost condition (2a) *"the same came to Jesus by night"*

III.   The truth of Christ is overwhelming to them (2b) *"for no man can do these miracles . . . except God be with him"*

IV.   A genuine spiritual experience with Christ is foreign to them (3) *"Except a man be born again, he cannot see the kingdom of God"*

V.   They are ignorant of the most elementary spiritual principles (4) *"How can a man be born when he is old?"*

In this example I chose the theme *The Conduct of Lost Religious Leaders* but this is not to say that I could not have used another. This particular method requires you to adjust your theme for the best results. If I were using the

130

expository method I would have used *The Spiritual Quest of a Lost Religious Leader*. That gives the best overall picture of what is happening in the passage. With the topical-textual sermon, however, you must word your theme in order to extract the inferences easily. If I had chosen the second theme above it would have made it more difficult even though it may have been possible.

It is easiest to draw inferences from a passage that depicts either something favorable on the one hand or unfavorable on the other. For example, Romans 8 speaks of the difficulty of waiting for our glorification. First Corinthians 5 reveals the ugly, carnal nature that is too often present in God's children. John 13 sheds light on the difficulty of an unconverted person to accept God's grace. John 3 depicts the cluelessness of a religiously lost person. These negatives are easily critiqued and the implications drawn from them will be used as the main divisions in a sermon body. It is harder to draw inferences from passages that do not clearly portray the positive or negative action of someone or something. This is not to say that it is impossible, it is just more difficult.

I laid great emphasis earlier on the importance of picking the right theme for a text. Historical narrative possesses the greatest degree of flexibility in choosing more than one theme. These alternative themes, however, will be closely related. For example, the theme *The Spiritual Quest of a Lost Religious Leader* and *The Conduct of Lost Religious Leaders* are similar. They both contain the essential motif of being a religious leader yet being lost. If your alternate themes are unrelated it is likely you are going off target. The point is that you have some flexibility depending upon what inferences you choose to stress.

Our final example will be a longer passage that everyone is familiar with: David and Goliath. Though this is much longer than the previous examples the principles remain the same whether drawing inferences from only a few verses or many.

Example: 1 Sam. 17

Theme   Characteristics of a Giant Killer (NKJV)
Main Divisions:

    I. Giant killers are insignificant by the world's standards (14-15) *"And David was the youngest ... and returned from Saul to feed his father's sheep at Bethlehem"*

    II. Giant killers have great interest in things that matter (22) *"David left his carriage . . . and ran into the army and saluted his brethren"*

    III. Disgrace is not an option for Giant killers (26) *"What shall be done to the man that taketh away the reproach from Israel?"*

    IV. Giant killers are jealous of God's honor above all (26) *"who is this uncircumcised Philistine, that he should defy the armies of the living God?"*

    V. Giant killers are not dissuaded by criticism (28-29) *"Eliab heard when he spake and his anger was kindled against David, and said, Why camest thou down hither? And David said," Is there not a cause?"*

    VI. Giant killers are concerned about the welfare of others (32) *"And David said to Saul, Let no man's heart fail because of him; thy servant will go and fight with this Philistine."*

VII. Giant killers rest on God's faithfulness of the past (37) *"The LORD that delivered me out of the paw of the lion, and out of the paw of the bear, he will deliver me out of the hand of this Philistine."*

VIII. Giant killers do not trust carnal means (39) *"David girded his sword upon his armour and said, I cannot go with these; for I have not proved them. And David put them off him."*

IX. To a giant killer little is much if God is in it (40) *"and chose him five smooth stones out of the brook, and put them in a shepherd's bag and his sling was in his hand."*

X. Giant killers depend on the strength of the Lord and not in themselves (45) *"Thou comest to me with a sword, and with a spear, and with a shield: but I come to thee in the name of the LORD of hosts, the God of the armies of Israel, whom thou hast defied."*

XI. Giant killers display amazing courage in the day of battle (46-48) *"I will smite thee, and take thine head from thee . . . David hastened, and ran toward the army to meet the Philistine."*

XII. Giant killers kill giants (49) "And David took thence a stone, and slang it, and smote the Philistine in his forehead, that the stone sunk into his forehead."

XIII. Giant killers instill great courage in others (52) *"And the men of Israel and of Judah arose, and shouted, and pursued the Philistines."*

THE TOPICAL EXPOSITORY SERMON:
The Applicatory Sermon

The topical-expository sermon is another hybrid sermon type falling under the general classification of biblical exposition. Its similarity to the topical-textual sermon (previous section) is immediately apparent. In the topical-textual sermon the preacher draws inferences from the text and unites those inferences into a theme. It is sometimes called the inferential sermon. The topical-expository sermon, however, is not so much concerned with making inferences as it is making applications. The difference between the two is not very great but warranted enough to make a distinction between the two sermon types.

If a passage is dealing with anything other than a particular personality then often it will yield inferences more than applications. If the passage, on the other hand, is biographical narrative it is more likely to yield applications instead of inferences. This is not a hard-and-fast rule. Only the context will dictate whether it is best to make inferences or applications. Topical-exposition, therefore, is especially useful for passages that are biographical that one can make applications to his own personal life. In order to understand the topical-expository sermon better we will contrast it with both the topical-textual and the traditional expository sermon approaches.

The traditional expository sermon uses a key noun to create a main division each time there is a change in subject matter in the text. This key noun will serve to qualify the overall theme in some respect. The key noun can be taken directly from the text or a dynamic equivalent can be substituted in its place. In either case it represents the biblical author's intentions exactly. Unlike the expository sermon the topical-textual sermon does not attempt to represent the biblical author's exact meaning. Instead it makes inferences about that text. For example, using 1 Cor. 5:1:

It is reported commonly that there is fornication among you, and such fornication as is not so much as named among the Gentiles, that one should have his father's wife.

The theme of 1 Cor. 5 is *Immorality in the Corinthian Church*. If we were to create an expository sermon out of this passage our first main division could be *The Severity of Immorality in the Church*. Verse one clearly states that the Corinthians were flirting with serious sin. The expository sermon plan simply states what the text is saying. The topical-textual sermon, however, draws inferences from it. The first main division, therefore, of a topical-textual sermon plan could be *The Sin of Believers is Often Worse Than the Sin of the World*. This is an inference but it is not an application. Since this passage is doctrinal and not biographical it makes more sense to make an application rather than an inference. This is where the two approaches differ.

I Kings 13 will serve as a good example of the usefulness of the topical-expository sermon. The passage depicts a bona fide prophet of God who was summoned to cry against the altar of King Jeroboam because of his idolatry. The prophet was divinely warned neither to eat or drink in that place nor to return back the way he came. After successfully crying out against Jeroboam's sinful altar another, older prophet living in that vicinity was determined to have this man come and eat with him at his house. Initially the prophet refused informing the older prophet of his divine mandate. The older prophet then lied telling the younger prophet that he had new revelation given to him by an angel of God allowing him to dine with him. To his own demise the younger prophet believed him and that decision cost him his life. Depending on what aspect of the story you choose to stress its theme will vary accordingly. I chose to concentrate on the older prophet's pathetic craving to be bona fide like his younger counterpart. I will use the theme, therefore, *Disobedient Preachers!*

These are the steps to take when creating a sermon from topical-exposition. This method here in *Thematic Preaching* comes from my professor of homiletics, Dr. J. L. Benson.[14]

1. Decide upon a theme that will determine the spiritual direction the sermon will go.
2. Using your own words or the words of the text itself, list all the statements in the passage that you intend to use to make the applications.
3. Using these statements, make those relevant applications.
4. Find the applications that relate to your theme and use them as your main divisions.

Let's go through the steps using I Kings 13.

1) Theme: Disobedient Preachers (NKJV)
2) Scriptural Statements:

1. Now an old prophet dwelt in Bethel (11)
2. his sons came and told him all the works that the man of God had done that day in Bethel (11)
3. "Which way did he go?". . . and went after the man of God . . . Then he said to him, "Come home with me and eat bread" (14-15)
4. He said to him, "I too am a prophet as you are, and an angel spoke to saying, 'Bring him back with you'" (He was lying to him.) (18)

---

[14] Benson, 95-101.

5. So he went back with him, and ate bread in his house, and drank water. (19)
6. Now it happened that the word of the Lord came to the prophet who had brought him back "Thus says the Lord: 'Because you have disobeyed . . . your corpse shall not come to the tomb of your fathers.'" (20-22)
7. And the prophet took up the corpse of the man of God . . . to mourn, and to bury him . . . saying, "Alas, my brother!" (29-30)
8. . . . the saying which he cried out against the altar in Bethel will surely come to pass (31-32)

3) Relevant Applications:

1. As this prophet was old, so also many called preachers are spiritually dried up
2. As this prophet only heard of God's work, so too, many preachers haven't seen the Spirit move in a long time in their own ministries
3. As this old prophet was obsessed with a bona fide prophet, so also disobedient preachers are obsessed with the success of obedient men of God
4. As this old prophet felt no shame for lying, so disobedient preachers have no problem sinning if it means personal gain for them
5. As this prophet was successful in turning the bona fide prophet from his mission, so disobedient preachers are successful in hindering the work of the ministry.

6. As this old prophet received a genuine word from the Lord, so the only time truth comes from disobedient preachers is when they are condemning someone else's sin, especially when they are to blame
7. As this old prophet felt remorse for the great harm he caused, so disobedient preachers mourn only after they have caused great harm and when it is too late
8. As this old prophet believed God's truth, even so disobedient preachers, ironically, respect God's word

4) The Sermon Plan:

Theme   Disobedient Preachers
Type   Topical Exposition
Main Divisions:

I.   Are spiritually dried up (11)
II.   Are no longer used by God (11)
III. Have an ungodly preoccupation with obedient servants of God (14-15)
IV.   Purposely and deceptively hinder the work of God's servants (18)
V.   Will be the first to condemn you when you err (20-22)
VI.   Mourn for the damage they cause only after it's too late (29-30)
VII. Cause confusion by mingling disobedience with the truth (31-32)

Example: Gen. 19 (NKJV)

Theme   The Conduct of a Carnal Christian
Statements:

1. Lot was sitting in the gate of Sodom (1)
2. Here now . . . please turn in to your servant's house and spend the night (2)
3. Please, my brethren, do not do so wickedly! (7)
4. See now, I have two daughters . . . please, let me bring them out to you, and you may do to them as you wish (8)
5. "Get up, get out of this place!" . . . But to his sons-in-law he seemed to be joking (14)
6. And while he lingered (15)
7. Escape to the mountains, lest you be destroyed . . . Please, no, my lords (17-18)
8. I cannot escape to the mountains, lest some evil overtake me and I die (19)
9. See now, this city is near enough to flee to, and it is a little one; please let me escape there (20)
10. I will not overthrow this city for which you have spoken. Hurry, escape there (21-22)
11. I cannot do anything until you arrive there (22)
12. So they made their father drink wine that night (33)
13. Thus both the daughters of Lot were with child by their father. . . Moab . . . Ammon (36-38)

Relevant Applications:

1. Just as Lot lived in sinful place, so carnal Christians fraternize with the world (*Statement #1*)
2. Carnal Christians are so starved for true fellowship that when it comes it is overwhelming to them (*Statement #2*)

3. Carnal Christians vex themselves with the company they keep (*Statement #3*)
4. Carnal Christians injure those they love (*Statement #4*)
5. The warning given by carnal Christians cannot be taken seriously by the world (*Statement #5*)
6. Carnal Christians are not concerned about the coming judgment of God (*Statement #6*)
7. Carnal Christians always provide an excuse for their sinful behavior (*Statements #7 & #8*)
8. Carnal Christians will always take the easy way out (*Statement #9*)
9. Carnal Christians get in the way of God's plan for this world (*Statements #10 & #11*)
10. Carnal Christians yield to temptation easily (*Statement #12*)
11. The legacy of carnal Christians will always be at war with the plan of God (*Statement #13*)

Sermon Plan:

Theme   The Conduct of Carnal Christians
Type   Topical Expository
Main Divisions:

I. Carnal Christians love the world (1)
II. Carnal Christians have little fellowship with believers (2)
III. Carnal Christians vex themselves with the company they keep (7)
IV. Carnal Christians injure those closest to them (8)
V. Carnal Christians are a joke to the world (14)

VI.   Carnal Christians are not concerned with God's coming judgment (15)

VII.   Carnal Christians always provide an excuse for their sinful behavior (18-19)

VIII.   Carnal Christians have no spiritual backbone (20)

IX.   Carnal Christians yield to temptation easily (33)

X.   Carnal Christians' legacies are at war with the plan of God (36-38)

As you review these last two hybrid sermon types you will notice that they are very close to one another. If you get confused do not worry about erring by crossing the line from one type to the other. The steps in both are virtually the same. The truths they yield are similar so there is no need for concern about the technical differences between the two. Sometimes an inference is almost the same as an application.

CHAPTER SIX

Biblical Genre, Literary Analysis, and   Discourse Analysis

THE DEFINITION OF BIBLICAL GENRE

A Biblical genre is a classification of Bible literature according to literary genre. The genre of a particular Bible passage is ordinarily identified by analysis of its general writing style, tone, form, structure, literary technique, content, design, and related linguistic factors; texts that exhibit a common set of literary features (very often in keeping with the writing styles of the times in which they were written) are together considered as belonging to a genre. In Biblical studies, genres are usually associated with whole books of the Bible, because each of its books comprises a complete textual unit; however, a book may be internally composed of a variety of styles, forms, and so forth, and thus bear the characteristics of more than one genre (for example, chapter 1 of the Book of Revelation is prophetic/visionary; chapters 2 and 3 are similar to the epistle genre; etc.).[15]

As usual Wikipedia does an apt job of explaining the subject matter at hand: In this case biblical genre. One of the greatest improvements over the past twenty-five years in the field of biblical studies, particularly with respect to hermeneutics (and even more recently with homiletics), has been the roles that literary analysis and genre play. David Robertson called this change of emphasis a "paradigm shift" noting the impact it has had on these two fields of study. [16] Formerly scholars and exegetes concerned themselves primarily with the grammar and history of the text. Literary matters were not important to

---

[15] Wikipedia, *Biblical Genre,* http://en.wikipedia.org/wiki/Biblical_genre (accessed June 25, 2012).
[16] David Robertson, *The Bible as Literature.*, Supplementary Volume, Keith Crim, ed., The Interpreter's Dictionary of the Bible, (Nashville: Abington Press, 1976), 547-551.

them until their value became too apparent to ignore. Sydney Greidanus explains its usefulness:

Literary analysis aids preachers in detecting the particular theme of a passage. The repetition of a word, phrase, clause, or action is frequently a clue to the theme. A chiastic structure usually focuses on the pivotal thought around which the passage turns. Again, a character's speech or narrator's point of view or comments may reveal a theme.[17]

Perhaps someone in the future will write an exhaustive treatise on the relationship between a homiletical outline and literary analysis. To my knowledge there are no "systems" that have been created. Diagrammatical analysis uses grammatical diagramming in order to create the main divisions of an outline but there are no systems that utilize literary analysis in the same fashion. There are some principles but nothing specific and uniform. This book attempts to make a good crack at exploring those possibilities.

The study of genre and literary analysis is essential to discovering the meaning of a text. For example, Psalm 103:3 states, *"Who forgiveth all thine iniquities; who healeth all thy diseases. "* Is this a specific promise that church saints can claim as a fool-proof formula for healing? Understandably many have hoped it meant this when faced with a life-threatening disease. Is this what the text is actually implying though? Or, is it a general truth that God often delivers us from diseases as well as many other unforeseen calamities that we are not even aware

---

[17] Sidney Greidanus, *The Value of a Literary Approach for Preaching*, A Complete Literary Guide to the Bible, ed. Leland Ryken and Tremper Longman III (Grand Rapids: Zondervan Publishing House, 1993), 512.

of? The answer to this lies in what classification of genre it falls under.

If this statement was recorded in a New Testament epistle we would have no choice but to interpret it literally (unless the context clearly dictated otherwise). However, this verse is written in the Psalms. Psalms, Lamentations, and the Song of Solomon fall into the category of genre called *Psalms*. Poetic statements in this genre, albeit precious, are not intended to be used as formulas for healing and deliverance but rather as general truths of God's faithfulness and righteousness. His faithfulness and righteousness, however, are the grounds in which we base our hope. They are intended to give us hope that He is, indeed, capable of healing us if it is His will as He has healed us in the past. This genre does not warrant interpreting it any other way. A novice at reading the Bible might not understand this and become severely disappointed if he claimed these statements as infallible promises in spite of the contextual meaning to the contrary.

CLASSIFICATIONS OF BIBLICAL GENRE

The following are the generally recognized genres and categorizations of the Bible (systems of classifications may vary):[18]

Historical narrative/epic: Genesis and the first half of Exodus, Numbers, Joshua, Judges, Ruth, 1 and 2 Samuel, 1 and 2 Kings, 1 and 2 Chronicles, Ezra, Nehemiah, Esther, Jonah, and possibly Acts

Law: the last half of Exodus; also Leviticus, Deuteronomy

---

[18] Wikipedia, *Biblical Genre*.

Wisdom: Job, Proverbs, Ecclesiastes

Psalms: Psalms, Song of Solomon, Lamentations

Prophecy: Isaiah, Jeremiah, Ezekiel, Daniel, Hosea, Joel, Amos, Obadiah, Jonah, Micah, Nahum, Habakkuk, Zephaniah, Haggai, Zechariah, Malachi

Apocalyptic: Daniel, Revelation

Gospel: Matthew, Mark, Luke, John

Epistle (letter): Romans, 1 and 2 Corinthians, Galatians, Ephesians, Philippians, Colossians, 1 and 2 Thessalonians, 1 and 2 Timothy, Titus, Philemon, Hebrews, James, 1 and 2 Peter, 1, 2, and 3 John, Jude

LITERARY ANALYSIS AS A MEANS OF BIBLICAL EXPOSITION

In his book God, Language, and Scripture, Moise's Silva does an absolutely masterful job of illustrating the importance that literary analysis plays in understanding a passage of Scripture. Literary analysis is a key component of determining which classification of genre a Bible book belongs to. As you can see from his example of historical narrative below his analysis lends itself very well to *Thematic Preaching.*

The story of the Tower of Babel (Gen. 11:1-9) stands as one of the most carefully crafted pieces of narrative in the book of Genesis. The passage naturally divides into two balanced sections, the first announcing what man proposed (vv. 1-4), the second declaring what God disposed (vv. 5-9). The contrast between the two sections is heightened by mockery. In place of stone and mortar, fragile brick with tar was used by these wicked and foolish people (v. 3). Their summons, "Come, let us build" is echoed in God's response, "Come, let us go down" (v. 7). They desired a great name, but the name their city received – which sounds like the Hebrew word for "confusion," babel –

was laughable. Their grand purpose was protection lest they be scattered over the earth, yet "the Lord scattered them over the face of the whole earth" (vv. 8-9). An Israelite listening to the story would have smiled with amusement from the very point where the wicked men began to speak, since the choice of words with a high frequency of the consonants b and l (habba nilbenah, "Come, let us make bricks" [v. 3]) anticipates the end of their designs.[19]

Moise's Silva makes outlining Gen. 11:1-9 easy:

Example: Gen. 11:1-9

Theme   The Story of the Tower of Babel: *When God Outwits Man's Evil Designs*

Type   Biblical Exposition/Literary Analysis

Main Divisions:

    I.   Its Sections
        1. What Man Proposed (1-4)
        2. What God Disposed (5-9)
   II.   Its Contrasts
        1. The contrast of building materials
           (1) Faulty material: Brick and tar (3a)
           (2) Appropriate material: Stone and mortar (3b)
        2. The contrast of summonses
           (1) Wicked man: "Come, let us build" (4)
           (2) God: "Come, let us go down" (7)
        3. The contrast of desires
           (1) Man: They desired a great name (4b)
           (2) God: They received another name: Babel (8)

---

[19]Moise's Silva, <u>God, Language, and Scripture</u>, in <u>Foundations of Contemporary Interpretation</u>, vol. 4, ed. Moises Silva (Grand Rapids: Zondervan Publishing House, 1990), 27.

4. The contrast of purposes
    (1) Man: They wanted protection from being scattered (4c)
    (2) God: "So the LORD scattered them abroad" (8)
III. Its Irony
    1. The irony of their beginning: "Come, let us make bricks" (v. 3), full of the consonants 'b' and 'l' i.e. *babel*
    2. The irony of their end: "and there confuse their language" (v. 7), i.e. A play on words: the Hebrew word 'babel' sounds like 'confusion.'

Organizing the outline in this fashion is perfectly acceptable in spite of the fact that it is not the most common way of developing an expository outline. Nevertheless it is a legitimate way to break the passage up into its component parts using literary analysis as a tool. Notice that *Thematic Preaching* is versatile enough to incorporate this method of organization without compromising its essential tenets. Furthermore a preacher does not have to alter this outline in order to preach from it. The logic is obvious: The entire passage is addressed, the outline relates to its theme perfectly, the main divisions are parallel, and it is easy to make spiritual applications from it. Sidney Greidanus expresses the need for flexibility when creating outlines in cases like this:

Instead of slavishly trying to copy the form of the text, preachers should carefully examine the form of the text and allow its

characteristics and mood to shape the form of the sermon. Thus, if the
text is a narrative one can use the narrative form . . .etc. [20]

Thematic Preaching is versatile enough to employ Greidanus's suggestion. Its design is to be utterly faithful to the text but flexible enough to incorporate other manners of organization as well. Here is another example of organizing a sermon around its literary analysis. Keep in mind that the following examples are given to demonstrate the usefulness of this approach. I am not suggesting that this is the only or best manner of using biblical exposition.

Example: Rev. 12:1-8

And there appeared a great wonder in heaven; a woman clothed with the sun, and the moon under her feet, and upon her head a crown of twelve stars: 2 And she being with child cried, travailing in birth, and pained to be delivered. 3 And there appeared another wonder in heaven; and behold a great red dragon, having seven heads and ten horns, and seven crowns upon his heads. 4 And his tail drew the third part of the stars of heaven, and did cast them to the earth: and the dragon stood before the woman which was ready to be delivered, for to devour her child as soon as it was born. 5 And she brought forth a man child, who was to rule all nations with a rod of iron: and her child was caught up unto God, and to his throne. 6 And the woman fled into the wilderness, where she hath a place prepared of God, that they should feed her there a thousand two hundred and threescore days. 7 And there was war in heaven: Michael and his angels fought against the dragon; and the dragon fought and his angels, 8 And prevailed not; neither was their place found any more in heaven.

Theme   War in Heaven: *Satan's Last-Ditch Effort to*
             Unseat God
Type   Exposition/Literary Analysis
Main Divisions:

---

[20] Greidnanus, 516.

I.   Its Apocalyptic Genre
        1. Visionary: The writer pictures characters
            and events remote from everyday life
        2. Epic: Supernatural characters, celestial
            battle, and cosmic setting
        3. Narrative: The emphasis on action
            reveals this bias
        4. Summation: Features — such as dualism
            between good and evil, the visionary
            mode, the Messianic focus on Christ,
            animal symbolism, and numerology —
            demonstrate its apocalyptic nature
II.   Its Symbolism
        1. The literary indicator of the symbolism:
            "Sign"
        2. The examples of the symbolism
            1) The woman: Israel
                (1) References the woman in
                    Joseph's dream, Jacob's wife, the
                    mother of the 12 tribes
                (2) References the sun, moon, and
                    stars of Joseph's dream, the 12
                    tribes
            2) The Child: Christ
            3) The Dragon: Satan
            4) The Dragon's attempt to devour the
                child: Reenactment of the
                redemptive life and ascension of
                Christ
III.   Its Features
        1. It mingles the familiar with the strange
        2. It suggests mystery and transcendence

3. It awakens universal feelings
    1) Since childhood we have known that a dragon means trouble
    2) Symbolic color of red is associated with something sinister
4. It possesses parody
    1) Seven heads of the dragon and the lamb with the seven horns
    2) Dragon's ten horns equate with evil

IV. Its refutation of common misconceptions
1. Though it is strange, it is not unique in that it employs common strategies of narrative and poetry
2. It is not completely futuristic. From a chronological standpoint it is a flashback from the main action in Revelation
3. Its symbols are not primarily esoteric but are either familiar biblical allusions or universal archetypes
4. The passage is symbolic rather than literal, though it brings actual events to mind

This example comes from Leland Ryken's literary analysis of the book of Revelation.[21] I organized it according to his description and put it into outline form. Though longer and more didactic than Silva's example the reader can see the usefulness of this approach. Viewing Scripture from the standpoint of a literary analyst yields enlightening and

---

[21] Leland Ryken, *Revelation*, <u>A Complete Literary Guide to the Bible</u>, ed. Leland Ryken and Tremper Longman III (Grand Rapids: Zondervan Publishing House, 1993), 467-8.

helpful information that an expositor would otherwise overlook. This particular example would be better suited in a classroom setting as opposed to a church service, but it could be modified easily enough to use as a sermon as well.

DISCOURSE ANALYSIS AND EXPOSITORY PREACHING

Moise's Silva has more pertinent things to say regarding the role that discourse analysis (a branch of literary analysis) plays in understanding and interpreting Scripture:

Although I need not here catalog all the formal features that contribute to the unity of the paragraph, I must mention a technique that has received increasing attention among biblical scholars. It has been long noticed that short portions of discourse (even modern conversations) sometimes takes the form, A-B-B'-A', known as chiasm. Note Galatians 4:4-5:

A   *God sent his son*
    B   *born of woman, born under the law,*
    B'   *to redeem those under the law,*
A'   *that we might receive the full rights of sons.*

Lines A and A' parallel each other (we could say they form an inclusio), and so do B and B'. The pattern is very common in Hebrew poetry and is been clearly detected in larger units, not only consisting of a large paragraph but even containing many paragraphs within it.[22]

Silva implies that without even realizing it we often speak and write in a fashion that organizes our thoughts into parallel groups. He confirms that chiastic structure is a fact. The question we must ask, therefore, is what does it mean regarding interpreting the Bible and more pertinently what does it mean with respect to preparing sermons? While the purpose of this book is to teach the

---

[22] Silva, 122

methodology of *Thematic Preaching* interpreting Scripture accurately also plays an important role as well. The reason is that in order to organize a sermon we must use the right theme. In order to choose a theme we must interpret Scripture accurately. If chiasm plays a role in either respect then it is pertinent to mention here.

What does the chiastic structure of Gal. 4:4-5 tell us if anything? Lines A and A' are parallel with one another and form an inclusio (i.e. book ends that bracket a literary unit). That is, there is something about them that is common so that the reader will make a connection between them. They both speak of "sonship" from the divine standpoint as well as from the human standpoint. The implication is obvious: We need to become a son like Him.

In addition B and B' are parallel and indicate a commonality between them. That is, the law plays an important role in the process of our becoming a son. B and 'B' are placed in the center of the passage indicating their vital relationship to the theme. Jesus was sent by God and was born under the law (implying that he lived it perfectly) so that we might be redeemed from the law (implying we could not). In a nut shell we need to become bona fide sons of God but we cannot because of the law. Jesus, the true Son, made that possible by living up to the law's demands. The chiastic form of Gal. 4:4-5 tells us the relationships between these truths. A and A' stress the key elements of the verses thus revealing the theme while B and B' explicate that theme. Put simply I chose *Sonship through the Son* as the theme of the verses.

If we use *Sonship through the Son* how can we put these verses in outline form? There are a couple of possibilities depending on how the preacher wants to stress the points. The first is to organize it using the expository form of the "aspects of" approach.

Example: Gal. 4:4-5

Theme   Sonship through the Son
Type   Exposition
Main Divisions:

    I.   His Commission (4a) *"God sent His Son"*
    II.   His Position (4b) *"born under the law"*
    III.   His Function (5a) *"to redeem them those under the law"*
    IV.   His Adoption (5b) *"that we might receive the full rights (adoption) as sons"*

If we organize it this way we are giving both A and A' equal literary value with B and B'. This is not a problem if the preacher wants to address each point to the same extent. By the same token just because the main points appear equally important doesn't mean that the expositor must treat them that way. He can put as much or as little stress on each point as he chooses. This is where flexibility becomes apparent. God may be moving him to stress an aspect of the law (B and B') more than He wants him to stress an aspect of sonship (A and A'). As long as these sub points relate back to the theme it is permissible. Obviously they must relate or the audience will be lost because its thoughts are not logically following the text. You cannot isolate the thoughts from one another.

Although the chiastic structure warrants subordination linguistically it does not mean a preacher is bound to stress it accordingly. While they must remain in context subpoints sometimes deserve more attention than major points depending upon how the preacher feels the Spirit is leading him. Organizing the outline using the expository form of "aspects of" highlights the flexibility of *Thematic Preaching*. Discourse analysis is very helpful in revealing the theme of a passage and the relationship between the thoughts. The genius of *Thematic Preaching*, however, utilizes these benefits but is not restricted by its structure.

There is an alternate way of organizing this sermon should the preacher want to mimic the form of the chiastic structure (as far as outward appearance is concerned). We could organize the outline accordingly:

Theme   Sonship through the Son
Main Divisions:

    I.   The Mission of the Son (4a) *"God sent forth His son"*
          1. The position in His mission (4b) *"born under the law"*
          2. The purpose of His mission (5a) *"to redeem those under the law"*
    II.   The Merit of the Son (5b) *"that we might receive the full rights as sons"*

Whether an expositor chooses this outline or the previous one is arbitrary. Both actually say the same thing. Homiletical structure is different than the structure in either discourse analysis or exegesis. Homiletical structure, particularly with respect to expository preaching, must be more flexible to permit the preacher to stress what he

feels is relevant. It conforms to the rigid structures of the others but is not strait-jacketed by them. It respects the vital roles that these play yet permits the Spirit's freedom to stress the points He feels are relevant.

CHAPTER SEVEN

Expository Preaching From Each Genre

HISTORICAL AND BIOGRAPHICAL NARRATIVE

I introduced biblical exposition from historical narrative in chapter 4. It would be very beneficial to return and reread that chapter along with the examples I used because I will refer back to them in this chapter.

Historical narrative comprises the largest portion of Scripture in the Bible. Inevitably, therefore, a preacher will be faced with its unique characteristics as he attempts to organize sermons from it. Creating an outline in historical narrative is often slightly easier than the other genres. The reader must remember, however, that in spite of this fact the principles of *Thematic Preaching* remain the same for all the genres. There is no need to fear as though preaching from each genre means reinventing the wheel each time. There are some differences between them and we will handle those differences at the proper time but all the genres are subject to the same rules.

Some homileticians make a distinction between historical and biographical narrative. Biographical narrative is a division of historical narrative whereby the history of someone's life is recorded and emphasized in the biblical text. Pure historical narrative, on the other hand, stresses the events of history without concentrating on someone's life per se. It is not possible to record history without the people involved but the difference lies in biographical narrative's emphasis of a personality. Both historical and biographical narrative can be found in other genres as well and is not confined to those books of the Bible classified as historical narrative. The gospels, though categorized in the genre called *Gospels*, contain much historical and biographical narrative. They are classified differently for other literary reasons.

The purpose of chapter 1 was to give the reader practice in choosing the right theme for a biblical text. Recall the example I used in 2 Sam. 9:1-13 concerning King David showing mercy to Jonathan's son, Mephibosheth. Second Samuel 9 is biographical narrative and we noticed that there were a couple of possibilities regarding the theme. We could state the theme according to the simple historical fact: *David's Kindness to Mephibosheth*. Or, we could state the theme according to the spiritual principle we are trying to teach from it: *The Bestowal of God's Grace*. When I preached this sermon I chose to use the latter of the two approaches. I will demonstrate both but before doing so let's use an approach which we already looked at in chapter 5 if for no other reason than to show all the possibilities for this passage. The topical-textual sermon plan worked very well with this sermon.

Example: 2 Sam. 9:1-13

Theme   The Bestowal of God's Grace
Type   Topical Textual (Inferential)
Main Divisions:

I.   It is given on the merits of someone else (1,7)
        "And David Said unto him, Fear not: for I will surely shew thee kindness for Jonathan thy father's sake"

II.   It is given to those who are helpless (2-3)
        "Jonathan hath yet a son, which is lame on his feet"

III.   It is given to the most undeserving (4-8)

> *"And he (Mephibosheth) bowed himself, and said, What is thy servant, that thou shouldest look upon such a dead dog as I am"*

IV. It is given without limits (9-13)

    1. With respect to how God blesses us (9-10)

> *"I (King David) have given unto thy master's son (Mephibosheth) all that pertained to Saul and to all his house"*

    2. With respect to how God treats us (11-13)

> *"So Mephibosheth dwelt in Jerusalem: for he did eat continually at the king's table; and was lame on both his feet"*

Notice that each main division teaches a spiritual truth about the bestowal of God's grace. In fact, this particular sermon delivers a powerful message about God's gracious dealing with undeserving sinners. When an expositor chooses a theme accordingly he cuts through the chaff and goes right to the spiritual principle. Devising the theme this way makes the spiritual lessons impossible to overlook. When the preacher fails to make spiritual applications from the text he has only given a history lesson that most people are not interested in. The inferential method of devising the main divisions makes the spiritual truths come to the surface. Let's use another approach:

Theme   The Bestowal of God's Goodness
Type   Biblical Exposition/Biographical Narrative
Main Divisions:

I. The bestowal of God's goodness is vicarious (1,7)

    i.e. on the behalf of someone else

II. The bestowal of God's goodness is propitious (2-3)

    i.e. it is merciful

III. The bestowal of God's goodness is gracious (4-8) *i.e. it is given in spite of the fact that we don't deserve it*

IV. The bestowal of God's goodness is bounteous (9-13) *i.e. it is more than we can imagine*

    1. With respect to how God blesses us (9-10) *i.e. He gives us all things*

    2. With respect to how God feels about us (11-13) *i.e. we even sit at His table*

This looks like the "characteristics of" approach in the topical sermon plan. The biblical writers themselves organized their thoughts that are reflected in *Thematic Preaching*. Notice that I altered this outline slightly. I changed the theme from "God's Grace" to "God's Goodness." The reason is because point III would read "The Bestowal of God's Grace is Gracious," a little redundant. Now let's outline the sermon in the most common way of biblical exposition:

Theme   David's Kindness to Mephibosheth: *Dealing Graciously with the Undeserving*

Main Divisions:

  I. His request (1-2) *"Is there any left of the house of Saul that I may show him kindness?"*

  II. His recipient (3-5) *"Jonathan hath yet a son, which is lame on his feet"*

  III. His reason (6-7) *"for I will surely shew thee kindness for Jonathan thy father's sake"*

  IV. His range (9-13)

        1. He gave Mephibosheth everything (9-10) *"I (King David) have given unto thy master's son (Mephibosheth) all that pertained to Saul and to all his house"*

2.   He invited him to eat at his table daily (11-13) *"So Mephibosheth dwelt in Jerusalem: for he did eat continually at the king's table"*

The theme of this outline states the historical fact without alluding to the spiritual lessons behind it. Likewise, the main divisions are aspects of it and don't reveal very much by way of practical application. This manner of organization is usually easier in biblical exposition. The preacher must make it clear, however, what the purpose of his message and points is. It is a good idea to use a title or subtheme to let the audience know what direction the sermon will take. For example, as is portrayed above the subtheme of this outline is *Dealing Graciously with the Undeserving.* Each of the main points must be backed with a similar spiritual lesson. For example, the *Request* might be equated with God's longing to impart salvation to a lonely, lost world. The *Recipients* are the undeserving and helpless people like you and me. The *Reason* for the Lord's kindness is because Jesus made us acceptable through His blood. The *Range* of His kindness can be equated with Him giving us all things that pertain to life and godliness etc.

In a nut shell the truths of the passage remain the same but the manner of treating them is different. The above three sermon plans essentially say the same thing. Usually I prefer the method in the last example because it is the easiest. In this case, however, using the topical-textual method did the most justice to an incredibly powerful and illustrious picture of our salvation.

When addressing a biographical passage the easiest way to state the main divisions is to use the pronoun of the person involved. For example, our theme is *David's Kindness to Mephibosheth* and we state the divisions as follows: *His* Request, *His* Recipient, *His* Reason, and *His* Range. Placing emphasis on the main character of the passage (in this case, David) is the simplest way of creating main divisions. The sermon must be centered in some way on the main character but the spiritual applications should be easy to make. If using the pronoun does not work because the English seems either awkward or restrictive then another manner of stating it is possible: *The* request to show kindness, *The* recipient of his kindness, *The* reason for his kindness, and *The* range of his kindness. The expositor has the flexibility to use whatever wording he feels will work at the time. Here are some other outlines that I used when preaching through 1 and 2 Samuel.

This example is taken from 1 Samuel 28 where Saul consults a medium to find out the future because the Spirit of the Lord had forsaken him. You may find it beneficial to read the passage before examining the outline and see if you agree with my organization.

Example: 1 Sam. 28

Theme   Saul Consults a Medium: *Can a Man Go Too Far with God?*

Type   Exposition, Biographical Narrative

Main Divisions:

     I.   His Corrupt Condition (3-6)

          1. Determinedly frightened (5) *"he was afraid, and his heart trembled greatly"*

          2. Divinely forsaken (6) *"And when Saul inquired of the LORD, the LORD answered him not"*

II. His Diabolical Decision (6, 7-14)
1. His motivation (6) *"the LORD answered him not"*
2. His medium (7) *"Seek me a woman that hath a familiar spirit"*
3. His masquerade (8-11) *"And Saul disguised himself, and put on other raiment"*
4. His manifestation (12-14) *"An old man cometh up . . . And Saul perceived that it was Samuel"*

III. His Somber Situation (15-25)
1. His somber report (15-19) *"the Lord will deliver Israel with thee into the hand of the Philistines: and tomorrow shalt thou and thy sons be with me"*
2. His somber response (20-25) *"Then Saul fell straightway all along the earth, and was sore afraid . . . and there was no strength in him"*

This clever outline depicts the entire chapter recording Saul's ultimate demise in a manner that the congregation can follow and remember. Likewise, the alliteration makes it easy for the expositor to remember his next points without being glued to his notes. Notice that following the theme I inserted a title (in question form) which gives the audience an idea for the purpose of the sermon. The message centers on the reality that it is possible, in fact, to go too far with God without the possibility of returning in repentance. It is a sermon that warns of the danger of ignoring God's will. The biographical narrative exhorts us to be careful to obey the Lord fully with a whole heart.

This next example is taken from 2 Sam. 1 where David receives news from an Amalekite that Saul and Jonathan were killed in Battle. The Amalekite confesses to have finished Saul off as he laid dying, rousing David's anger to the extent of executing the young man for it.

Example: 2 Sam. 1:1-27

Theme   David's Grief for Saul and Jonathan:
                    Grieving for the Loss of a Loved One

Type   Exposition/Biographical Narrative

Main Divisions:

  I. His cross-examination (1-10) *"How went the matter?" i.e. the battle*

  II. His choler (13-16) *"How wast thou not afraid to stretch forth thine hand to destroy the Lord's anointed? . . . And he smote him that he died"*

  III. His cry (11-12, 17-27) *"And they mourned, and wept, and fasted"*

Each of the divisions above relate in some manner to grieving. It may not be apparent on the surface but the expositor can make spiritual and practical applications from each. When I preached this text I applied it to the issue of grieving over the loss of someone we love. We ask questions, we get angry, and we weep with sorrow. Although it is ancient history it reveals a part of human nature that hasn't changed since time began.

The next example demonstrates how simple it is to construct an outline that is coherent. You will notice that the thoughts are logical and simple to follow. Sometimes it is the best way of organizing a sermon when the truths are so plain. You don't always have to be fancy. The lack of alliteration might be a nice change for the audience. The context of this passage is when David desired to build the temple for the Lord but the Lord told him He would build him a house (dynasty) instead. In theological terms it is called the Davidic Covenant.

Example: 2 Sam. 7

Theme   The Davidic Covenant: *The Promises God Gave to David*
Type   Exposition, Historical Narrative
Main Divisions:

> I.   You will NOT build my house (1-7)
> II. Your name will be great (8-9)
> III. You and your people will have peace (10-11a)
> IV. I will build you a house (11b-16)

The next example is taken from 2 Samuel 16:1-14 when David was fleeing Jerusalem for his life because Absalom, his son, orchestrated a military coup against him. On the way out two evil men met him. The first one greeted him with gifts in order to turn David's heart away from his best friend's son so that he would give him his property. This becomes apparent in 19:25-30. The second one met him with curses because he hated David for taking the throne from Saul. Notice the ingenuity and colorfulness of this outline making it interesting to preach from.

Example: 2 Sam. 16:1-14

Please refer to this passage and then return here in order to study the outline for yourself

Theme   Trials Along the Way: *When it Rains, it Pours!*
Type   Biblical Exposition, Biographical Narrative
Main Divisions:

I.   Trial # 1: A Snake in the Grass: *A Test of Trust* (1-4)
1. The background of the snake (1)
2. The bribe of the snake (2)
3. The betrayal by the snake (3)
4. The bequest of the snake (4)

II.   Trial #2: A Serpent in the Way: *A Test of Humility* (5-14)
1. A rundown on the serpent (5-6)
    1) His identity (5)
    2) His insult (6)
    3) His imprecation (7-8)
2. A response to the serpent: David's godly attitude
    1) David's resignation (9-10)
    2) David's rationale (11-12)
    3) David's resolve (13-14)

There are several things to notice about the outline that are worth mentioning. For starters, the theme and subtheme indicate that the purpose of the sermon is to show how tough life can be sometimes. When it rains, it pours! When hardships come other unforeseen attacks and calamities accompany them. The outline completely reflects the practical and spiritual lessons inherent in this passage. In addition, subpoint II. 2., *A response to the serpent,* has a descriptive phrase following it: *David's godly attitude.* Occasionally it is necessary to use these additional phrases for clarification's sake. In this case it was not necessary but sometimes it is. If the wording of the main point is not clear enough for the audience to follow then the use of these additional, descriptive phrases is necessary. Furthermore, the descriptive phrase may be used as the primary division in place of the one it is clarifying. If it is not possible to retain parallel subdivisions using the main point then try using a descriptive phrase in its place. It may be easier to create subpoints from it.

You will also notice that I added a further statement to the two main divisions: *A Test of Trust* and *A Test of Humility*. These trials were also tests of David's character. The outline reflects this to let the congregation know the spiritual direction the sermon will take. Would he trust Mephibosheth or would he trust this snake who he didn't even know? Because David believed this liar he failed this test (see 2 Sam. 19:24). The second test was a trial of humility. David passed this test with flying colors by taking responsibility for the problems he faced and by not avenging himself with the execution of Shimea. He demonstrated that he was a man after God's own heart.

The next example from Gen.19:24-29 depicts the destruction of Sodom and Gomorrah because of their wickedness. This is an example of pure historical narrative without concentrating on one personality. The manner of treatment is very similar to biographical narrative with the exception that the main divisions center on something other than a person.

Example: Gen. 19:24-29

24 Then the Lord rained brimstone and fire on Sodom and Gomorrah, from the Lord out of the heavens. 25 So He overthrew those cities, all the plain, all the inhabitants of the cities, and what grew on the ground. 26 But his wife looked back behind him, and she became a pillar of salt. 27 And Abraham went early in the morning to the place where he had stood before the Lord. 28 Then he looked toward Sodom and Gomorrah, and toward all the land of the plain; and he saw, and behold, the smoke of the land which went up like the smoke of a furnace. 29 And it came to pass, when God destroyed the cities of the plain, that God remembered Abraham, and sent Lot out of the midst of the overthrow, when He overthrew the cities in which Lot had dwelt. (NKJV)

Theme   The Destruction of Sodom and Gomorrah:
                 Pay Day Some Day
Type   Exposition, Historical Narrative
Main Divisions:

I.   The Characteristics of the Destruction (24-28)
      1. It was a fierce destruction (24-25)
          1) Fierce for those filled with evil
              (1) A fierce means (24) *"fire and brimstone"*
              (2) A fierce end (25) *"*And He overthrew those cities*"*
          2) Fierce for those flirting with evil (26) *"but his wife looked back and became a pillar of salt"*
      2. It was final destruction (27-28) *"the smoke of the country went up as the smoke of a furnace"*

II.   The Clemency in the Destruction (29) *"when God destroyed the cities of the plain, that God remembered Abraham, and sent Lot out"*

This outline took a lot of work to perfect. Initially I was trying to break the passage up into four equal parts but couldn't do it if I wanted to use alliteration. I was forced to divide the outline into two major sections instead. It worked out better in the end because the points became more accurate and descriptive than if I presented it using four distinct major divisions. This brings up an interesting point: When an outline won't come together it is probably because there is a better way of organizing it. It takes a lot of flexibility and patience on the part of the expositor to acknowledge when he is beat and try something else. As the title implies the aim of this sermon is to warn that God will ultimately make good on His threats if sinners do not repent. It should stress the seriousness and urgency of impending judgment both on the hardened sinner and the saint who flirts with sin.

Before leaving historical and biographical narrative I want to give you one more example from a subgenre found occasionally in the midst of the major genres including here. It is oracle. The record of David's last words in 2 Samuel is a good example.

Example: 2 Sam. 23:1-7

Now these be the last words of David. David the son of Jesse said, and the man who was raised up on high, the anointed of the God of Jacob, and the sweet psalmist of Israel, said, 2 The Spirit of the Lord spake by me, and his word was in my tongue. 3 The God of Israel said, the Rock of Israel spake to me, He that ruleth over men must be just, ruling in the fear of God. 4 And he shall be as the light of the morning, when the sun riseth, even a morning without clouds; as the tender grass springing out of the earth by clear shining after rain. 5 Although my house be not so with God; yet he hath made with me an everlasting covenant, ordered in all things, and sure: for this is all my salvation, and all my desire, although he make it not to grow. 6 But the sons of Belial shall be all of them as thorns thrust away, because they cannot be taken with hands: 7 But the man that shall touch them must be fenced with iron and the staff of a spear; and they shall be utterly burned with fire in the same place.

Theme   David's Last Oracle: *A Contrast Between the Righteous and the Wicked*

Type   Exposition/Biographical Narrative/Oracle
Main Divisions:

    I.   His Self-Portrait (1)
        1. His position (1a-b)
        2. His inspiration (1b-c)
    II.   His Spiritual Provenance (2-3b)   *i.e. his spiritual source*
    III. His Sacred Proverb (3c-4)
        1. The marks of a godly ruler (3)
            1) Righteousness
            2) Reverence
        2. The metaphors of a godly ruler (4)
            1) Light
            2) Brightness
    IV. His Saintly Position: *The Davidic Covenant* (5)
        1. A personal covenant
        2. A permanent covenant
        3. A positive covenant
        4. A plentiful covenant
    V.   His Severe Pronouncement (6-7)
        1. The wicked are useless
        2. The wicked are injurious
        3. The wicked are hopeless

EXPOSITION FROM THE LAW GENRE

The Law genre consists of the second half of Exodus, Leviticus, and Deuteronomy. Most books of the Bible contain a mix of more than one genre but these three mentioned are typically characterized by legal stipulations and commands of the Mosaic Law. Analyzing this genre from a literary standpoint is advantageous not only because it lends itself to creating homiletical outlines (as we have seen in the earlier examples) but more importantly because literary analysis greatly assists the expositor in discovering the proper theme. As I stated earlier the theme is the glue that holds a sermon together. In the case of Law genre there are certain literary characteristics such as the stylistic arrangements of laws which are helpful for an expositor in developing his outline. Concerning these stylistic arrangements consider the following statements by the experts:

The laws or teachings begun in Exodus and concluded in Deuteronomy, then, are of two kinds, absolute . . ., usually introduced by the contrasting formulas "Thou shalt" or "Thou shalt not," and conditional ones . . ., expressed in a narrative form, such as "If a man [does this], then [this will happen]. . . Brief commands of this kind are often embellished by a positive/negative pattern. For example, the prescription "Judges and officers shalt thou make thee in all thy gates" is a positive command requiring judges in all cities in all the tribes to be "just", but this is followed by two negative warnings against favoritism and bribery and then by a final reminder to be "just" (Deut. 16:18-20). Thus, the law is given four times, developed by parallel negative statements in a parallel positive frame.[23]

The analysis above tells us some important things about Deut. 16 as well as the typical style of law-type Scripture. When we see commands that start with "Thou shalt" or "Thou shalt not" we know that these are absolute commands which are stylistically structured for emphasis. The negative aspects of the commandments are sandwiched between the positive ones in a parallel fashion that gives the passage unity and purpose. Literary analysis

---

[23] Wilson G. Baroody and William F. Gentrup, *Exodus, Leviticus, Numbers, Deuteronomy*, <u>A Complete Literary Guide to the Bible</u>, eds. Leland Ryken and Tremper Longman III (Grand Rapids: Zondervan Publishing House, 1993), 128-129.

tells us that the two positive commands reveal the theme while the negative ones embellish that theme. Let's take a look at Deut. 16:18-20 and see if this analysis helps us create an outline.

Example: Deut. 16:18-20

You shall appoint judges and officers in all your gates, which the Lord your God gives you, according to your tribes, and they shall judge the people with just judgment. 19 You shall not pervert justice; you shall not show partiality, nor take a bribe, for a bribe blinds the eyes of the wise and twists the words of the righteous. 20 You shall follow what is altogether just, that you may live and inherit the land which the Lord your God is giving you. (NKJV)

Theme   The Command to Appoint Just Judges
Type   Exposition/Law Genre
Main Divisions:

I.   The Distinctives of the Command (18)
   1.   It is unalterable (absolute) *"You shall"*
   2.   It is universal *"in all your gates . . . according to your tribes"*
   3.   It is unprejudiced *"they shall judge the people with just judgment"*

II.   The Deterrents to the Command (19)
   1.   Perverting justice
   2.   Showing partiality
   3.   Taking bribes
      1)   Bribes blind the eyes of the wise
      2)   Bribes twist the words of the righteous

III.   The Design of the Command (20)
   1.   It is designed to guide us *"You shall follow what is altogether just"*
   2.   It is designed to bless us *"that you may live and inherit the land"*

The literary analysis benefits us by telling us the nature of the command. That is, it is absolute. The structure reveals what the theme is: *Appointing Just Judges.* Furthermore it embellishes that theme by switching from the positive aspects to negative and back to positive. This A-B-A' structure is reflected in the outline above with the first and third positive divisions sandwiching the negative aspects between it. This pattern can be expected in the majority of cases in this genre.

There are other formats of structure which can be found in the law genre. Notice what the scholars say:

> Other series of laws are usually arranged to achieve variety by alternating absolute and conditional forms. Sometimes the conditional instructions are brief, and sometimes they treat a specific topic at length. Those found in Deuteronomy 22 are good examples. Observing the usual pattern, the passage starts with the absolute type of command (two in this case), followed by two conditional ones, then a series of absolute commands, and an even longer series of conditional ones; it concludes with a terse absolute command.[24]

The important thing to notice is that there is, in fact, structure involved with Moses' writings and it is by design. The expositor must recognize these stylistic patterns and arrange his outline while taking into account the important factors that literary analysis reveals. Notice in the example below that the structure of the outline is the same as those examples given earlier for biblical exposition. *Thematic Preaching* remains the same regardless of the specific genre. *Thematic Preaching* molds itself around the peculiarities of a certain genre but the principles, basically, remain unchanged.

---

[24] Baroody and Gentrup, 129.

Example: Deut. 20: 1-20

Please refer to this passage and then return here in order to examine the outline for yourself.

Theme   The Law of Warfare
Type   Exposition/Law genre
Main Divisions:

    I. Encouragement in Warfare (1-4)
    II. Exemptions in Warfare (5-9)
        1. Those who recently built a house (5)
        2. Those who recently planted a vineyard (6)
        3. Those who recently married or are about to (7)
        4. Those who are afraid (8)
    III. Etiquette in Warfare (10-20)
        1. Concerning the heathen (10-18)
            1) The heathen outside the borders of Israel (10-15)
            2) The heathen inside the borders of Israel (16-18)
        2. Concerning the hemlocks (19-20)

The theme in the above example is *The Law of Warfare* and must be treated in a similar manner to passages from historical narrative. The themes in both of these genres often need additional clarifying statements in order to point to the spiritual direction of the sermon. In other words the subject matter does not necessarily relate to everyday living. The expositor must take the subject matter and make it applicable to the person in the pew. The epistles, on the other hand, do not need this treatment. Their content is naturally applicable for today's living. By comparison historical narrative would be on one end of the spectrum and the epistles would be on the other. Law genre sits to the immediate right of historical narrative and frequently needs additional statements to aid the theme. That is, historical narrative and law genre often need a subtheme, title, or explanatory statement (some homileticians would also call this the propositional statement) to make the ancient customs and times relevant to the people today.

Developing a sermon from historical narrative, therefore, (and frequently Law genre) means that there may not always be a concise theme in the passage. In place of the theme the preacher must resort to using a simple, descriptive statement of the subject matter with no indication of a moral or spiritual lesson. For example, *Paul's Voyage to Rome* does not really fit the definition of a theme given in the first chapter. Some might argue that this is not a theme at all but only a basic summary of the contents. Regardless, as long as there is a subtheme or title to let the audience know what the spiritual direction the sermon will take there shouldn't be any problems. If the theme *Paul's Voyage to Rome* does not use a subtheme or title then the preacher is only giving a history lesson and the congregation will quickly grow weary.

On the other end of the spectrum are the epistles. By nature their subject matter involves spiritual application and therefore they usually do not need a subtheme or title. The theme from an epistolary text not only reveals the content but also indicates the spiritual direction the sermon will take. It is not history but doctrinal and practical mandates to live by. Somewhere in the middle of this spectrum lay the rest of the genres. Some very close to the epistles on the far right (such as the teachings of Jesus) and in this case Law, which is closer to historical narrative on the far left.

If an expositor used the above outline from Deuteronomy 20 he would have to make it relevant somehow to the congregation. These specific laws were given to a people long ago in a different dispensation. Are they applicable today? What correlations can we make with the teachings of Jesus or the epistles? If the laws are timeless in nature (this is also referred to as the moral aspect of the law) then they speak for themselves and might not need any sub theme or title. They would be on par with the epistles and would not need any creativity to make them applicable. If, on the other hand, they only apply to Israel then the expositor must make the relevant applications and correlations to New Testament principles. The Deut. 20 example would, indeed, require a subtheme/title because *"the weapons of our warfare are not carnal."* Christians are not mandated to physically kill anyone. Quite the contrary we are to kill them with truth and love. Hence the spiritual application is obvious.

BIBLICAL EXPOSITION FROM THE WISDOM GENRE

Job

Wisdom genre consists of three books: Job, Proverbs, and Ecclesiastes. No one argues whether Proverbs or Ecclesiastes belongs in this genre but Job, on the other hand, is a different story. Jerry Gladson, literary scholar, yields this insightful information:

The Joban author, as is generally the case with any writer, has drawn from a variety of genres to create a distinct composition. Within the

175

book there are several sub genres, e.g., narrative (chs. 1-2; 42:7-17), soliloquy (chs. 3, 29-31), a disputation (chs. 4-27), theophany (chs. 38-41), and the wisdom poem (ch. 28). Job participates in a variety of genres, none of which applied rigidly characterizes the entire book.[25]

Since we are dealing with several different subgenres the expositor must handle each of these individually. Take for example, soliloquy. A soliloquy is an *utterance or discourse by a person who is talking to himself or herself or is disregardful of or oblivious to any hearers present.*[26] Job does this in chapter 3 and also in chapters 29-31 while lamenting his mournful predicament. These verses are not easy to put into sermonic form. The method of outlining must be flexible enough to categorize the various sentiments into parallel and logical divisions.

Elmer B. Smick does a superb job of explaining the structure of chapter 3 in his commentary on Job which we will use here in order to diagram this passage.[27] He quotes other scholars giving credit for their contribution to the understanding of the literary unity of this text. One of those scholars, N.C. Habel,[28] created the following accurate depiction of the passage. As you read chapter 3

---

[25]Jerry A. Gladson, *Job*, A Complete Literary Guide to the New Testament, ed. Leland Ryken and Tremper Longman III (Grand Rapids: Zondervan Pub. House, 1993), 232.

[26]Dictionary.com. http://dictionary.reference.com/browse/soliloquy?s=ts (accessed July 2, 2012).

[27] Elmer B. Smick, *Job*, The Expositor's Bible Commentary, Vol. 4, ed. Frank E. Gaebelein (Grand Rapids: Zondervan Pub. House, 1988).

[28] N.C. Habel, *The Book of Job*, The Cambridge Bible Commentary on the N.E.B. (Cambridge: Cambridge University Press, 1975).

of Job in your Bible review this outline and notice the parallel divisions and coherence.

Example: Job 3

Theme   Job Grieves the Day of His Birth: *When We Just Can't Take It Anymore*

Type   Exposition/Wisdom/Soliloquy

Main Divisions:

    I.   The Curses
        1. Subject: Day and Night (vs. 3)
            1) Curses on that day (vv. 4-5)
            2) Curses on that night (vv. 6-9)
        2. Reasons for his curse: Misery (vs. 10)
    II.   The Lament
        1. Subject: Why he did not die at birth (vs. 11)
          • Laments on why God permits suffering (vv. 12-24)
        2. Reason for his lament (vv. 25-26)[29]

The important thing to notice in this outline is that the chapter naturally divides into two major sections: Curses and lament. It takes a keen eye to detect these two divisions amidst a lot of similar sounding, repetitive phrases and poetic statements. The language is nothing like the epistles where the change of subject matter is easy to pinpoint. Since there are no doctrinal points, historical/biographical content, or other easily noticeable contrasts in subject matter a preacher must use other methods of analysis when dealing with genres that do not

---

[29]Smick, 890.

lend themselves easily to outline form. This is where the aid of literary analysis is beneficial.

A person does not have to be a literary scholar to create such outlines but he does have to change his mindset and abandon the more traditional, rigid methods of sermon preparation if he is going to do justice to genres of Scripture like this one. He must be able to discern the way Job uses language and expresses himself rather than pinpointing obvious transitions into new material. The language of soliloquy is not written to teach or give information but to express how one feels. Without noticing these subtle shifts of emotions the expositor is paralyzed as he attempts to create an outline that makes sense. Diagrammatical analysis and other traditional methods of sermon preparation, in spite of their notable contributions to the field of homiletics, are of no benefit when it comes to the more difficult subgenres like soliloquy.

When stating the theme of a sermon the expositor must make applications to ordinary life. It's fine to create an accurate, concise outline which aptly describes the content of the passage but how does this relate to an average person in the pew? I supplied the theme to the previous example because the original author of the outline did not have one. Notice that I also added the descriptive phrase *When We Just Can't Take it Anymore!!* This gives the audience a clue as to where the sermon is going.

Other than the title and theme that I supplied this outline is not quite sufficient to preach from because it needs to be modified in order to make spiritual applications. The author's intention, of course, was to analyze the passage from a literary standpoint, not to preach a sermon. We can employ, however, his analysis and modify it for the pulpit. The aspiring preacher should not feel overwhelmed thinking that literary analysis is beyond his reach of comprehension. A worthwhile investment for any expositor of the Word of God is several good books on the subject of the literary analysis of the Bible. I found the above outline by browsing several such sources.

Disputation is the next genre in Job (a subgenre of wisdom literature) spanning chapters 4-27. Elmer B. Smick quotes F.I. Anderson[30] who analyzes the first of Eliphaz's speeches (chapters 4-5) giving the following insight:

A. Opening (4:2)
B. Exhortation (4:3-6)
C. God's Dealings with Men (4:7-11)
D. Revelation of Truth (12-21)
C'. God's Dealings with Men (5:1-16)
B'. Exhortation (5:17-26)
A'. Closing Remark (5:27)[31]

This analysis reveals that Eliphaz's speech is a well-crafted literary unit wherein the divisions are logically broken up into their respective parts. If an expositor is going to preach this passage from Job then understanding its organizational structure is imperative. Each of these divisions could be preached individually or combined into bigger units. Within each of these sections is its own form

[30] F. I. Anderson, Job: An Introduction and Commentary (Downers Grove, Ill.: Intervarsity Press, 1976).
[31] Smick, 897.

and structure which the expositor must discover as he breaks the passage apart further. The above major divisions are not, unfortunately, suitable to preach from. The only thing the analysis reveals is the progression of thought of the speaker, Eliphaz. Understanding the literary structure is absolutely essential, however, if an expositor is going to preach through the book of Job. The nature of expository preaching is to be able to trace the biblical writer's own progression of thought and then create a sermonic outline from it.

Keep in mind that genres found in Job (as well as in other books in the Bible particularly in the OT) will frequently take their own form as opposed to the more common genres such as historical narrative or epistolary. How is an expositor going to handle Eliphaz's speech? Preaching from only a few verses may be difficult at times because there is not enough information. The volume of words is poetic in nature.

Occasionally the best method is to preach an entire passage in one sermon. Admittedly, however, this would be difficult to do with the above example. In cases where it is beneficial the preacher would choose several key verses of each section and make the main divisions and spiritual applications. It would not be necessary to expound every verse. *Thematic Preaching* is flexible enough to adapt to such an approach. Preaching successfully from a large portion of Scripture is an art in itself. Once the outline is crafted it would be advisable for the preacher to go over the sermon numerous times in order to get a handle on what he is dealing with before the actual delivery. He must make sure that his major divisions relate to a good theme and that he is not covering too much information. He must make a large biblical text seem small. I have had some success doing this but it is certainly neither easy nor always advisable.

Below is my attempt at creating a sermonic outline of Eliphaz's first speech found in Job 4 and 5. I am only using the first 11 verses of chapter 4 because there is sufficient information to expound. The theme of Eliphaz's first speech could be *The Admonition of a Hypocrite*. Each sermon preached from these 48 verses must use the same theme but with, of course, a different sermon body and emphasis. Here is my first sermon outline:

Example: Job 4:1-11

Then Eliphaz the Temanite answered and said, 2 If we assay to commune with thee, wilt thou be grieved? but who can withhold himself from speaking? 3 Behold, thou hast instructed many, and thou hast strengthened the weak hands. 4 Thy words have upholden him that was falling, and thou hast strengthened the feeble knees. 5 But now it is come upon thee, and thou faintest; it toucheth thee, and thou art troubled. 6 Is not this thy fear, thy confidence, thy hope, and the uprightness of thy ways? 7 Remember, I pray thee, who ever perished, being innocent? or where were the righteous cut off? 8 Even as I have seen, they that plow iniquity, and sow wickedness, reap the same. 9 By the blast of God they perish, and by the breath of his nostrils are they consumed. 10 The roaring of the lion, and the voice of the fierce lion, and the teeth of the young lions, are broken. 11 The old lion perisheth for lack of prey, and the stout lion's whelps are scattered abroad.

Theme   Admonition of a Hypocrite: Part I
Type   Expository/wisdom genre/disputation
Main Divisions:

      I.   His Aspiration (1-2) i.e. *His desire to admonish Job*

    1. His carefulness (2) *"If we assay to commune with thee, wilt thou be grieved?"*
    2. His candor (2) *"But who can withhold himself from speaking?"*

II. His Exhortation (3-6)
    1. His exhortation about Job's past (3-4) *"thou hast instructed . . ." etc.*
    2. His exhortation about Job's present (5) *"it is come upon thee" etc.*
    3. His exhortation about Job's future (6) *"Is not this thy fear, thy confidence, thy hope..."*

III. His Supposition (7-11)
    1. The presentation of his supposition (7) *"Remember now, whoever perished being innocent?"*
    2. The principle behind his supposition (8) *"they that plow iniquity, and sow wickedness, reap the same"*
    3. The punishment in his supposition(9-11)
       1) The intensity of the punishment (9) *"By the blast of God they perish"*
       2) The illustration of the punishment (10-11) *"lion"*
          (1) Young lions: teeth broken
          (2) Old lions: perish for lack of prey
          (3) Lionesses: cubs are scattered

A few things to notice about this outline are first and foremost that the three main divisions follow the literary breakdown. (See F.I. Anderson's literary breakdown given earlier in this section, i.e. opening, exhortation, God's dealing with men). Having created the proper theme, *Admonition of a Hypocrite*, I then proceeded to make the main divisions by using a key noun that described the content of the related verses. This format follows the typical "aspects of" that we were first introduced to in the topical sermon section. Sometimes this simple breakdown will not be that easy.

The following outline is adapted from Smick's commentary on Job. The Lord's speeches are the last section of the book of Job. As you can see the manner of treatment is not that much different from the previous example.

Example: Job 38:2-39:30

Theme   Lord of All
Type: Exposition/wisdom/theophany
Main Divisions:

    I.   Lord Over His Subjects (38:2-3)
         1. He impugns them (2)
         2. He interrogates them (3)
    II.   Lord Over Creation (4-15)
         1. Creator of the earth (4-7)
         2. Creator of the sea (8-11)
         3. Creator of the day and night (12-15)
    III.   Lord Over Nature (38:16-39:30)
         1. Lord over inanimate nature (38:16-38)
            1) The depths and expanses (16-18)
            2) Light and darkness (19-21)
            3) Weather (22-30)
            4) Stars (31-33)
            5) Floods (34-38)
         2. Lord over animate nature (38:39- 39:30)
            1) Nourishment (39-41)
            2) Procreation (39:1-4)
            3) Wild freedom (5-8)
            4) Intractable strength (9-12)

5) Incongruous speed (13-18)
6) Fearsome strength (19-25)
7) Flight from the predator (26-30)[32]

Proverbs

Most of the proverbs are single, literary units contained in one verse. Sometimes a proverb may constitute two or three verses and occasionally even more (e.g. 24:30-34). Organizing the proverbs into sermonic form can take a few different avenues. First, each proverb can be dealt with individually much like the textual method of sermon preparation. Parallel statements within the proverb would constitute the main divisions of the outline. Another method is to pick a particular proverb and expound it using other similar proverbs that state the same truths. For example, if we choose a theme such as *The Actions of a Lazy Man* we could find several different things that sluggards are noted for. For example, a lazy man sleeps (6:9), begs (20:4), argues (26:16), desires (13:4), and vexes (10:26). This simple approach can be used throughout the book of Proverbs. Below is an example using the standard textual method.

Example: 11:10

When it goeth well with the righteous, the city rejoiceth: and when the wicked perish, there is shouting.

Theme   Two Reasons Why People Rejoice
Type   Textual/Proverb
Main Divisions:

I.   Reason #1: When it Goes Well With the Righteous

---

[32] Smick, 1034.

II. Reason #2: When the Wicked Perish

Although it may seem unusual to preach an outline this short and sweet an expositor certainly could. Needless to say he would have to supply a lot of information to the body of sermon such as other pertinent verses, stories, or personal experience.

Example: Prov. 25:9-10

Debate thy cause with thy neighbour himself; and discover not a secret to another: Lest he that heareth it put thee to shame, and thine infamy turn not away.

Theme   The Wisdom of Confidentiality
Type   Textual/Wisdom/Proverb
Main Divisions:

I.   The Mandate for Confidentiality
   1.   A mandate for personal discussions *"Debate thy cause with thy neighbour himself"*
   2.   A mandate for private discussions *"discover not a secret to another"*

II.   The Mousetrap of Confidentiality
   1.   Trapped in shame *"put thee to shame"*
   2.   Trapped in name *"and thine infamy turn not away"*

Example: 24:30-34

30 I went by the field of the slothful, and by the vineyard of the man void of understanding; 31 And, lo, it was all grown over with thorns, and nettles had covered the face thereof, and the stone wall thereof was broken down. 32 Then I saw, and considered it well: I looked upon it, and received instruction. 33 Yet a little sleep, a little slumber, a little folding of the hands to sleep: 34 So shall thy poverty come as one that travelleth; and thy want as an armed man.

Theme	Warnings Against Sloth
Type	Expository/Wisdom/Proverb
Main Divisions:	

    I.   The Illustration of Sloth: *A Vineyard* (30-31)
        1. The proprietor of the vineyard (30)
            1) He was idle
            2) He was idiotic
        2. The predicament of the vineyard (31)
            1) Overgrown with thorns
            2) Nettles covered the face of it
            3) Stone wall broken down
    II. The Instructions of Sloth (32-34)
        1. Sloth is self-evident (32) *"I looked upon it, and received instruction"*
        2. Sloth is subtle (33) *"Yet a little sleep, a little slumber"*
        3. Sloth is severe (34) *"and thy want as an armed man"*

Ecclesiastes

I alluded to the fact that to preach an expository sermon is to understand the theme and progression of thought of the passage. If an expositor cannot discern the overall theme of the book he is preaching through then how can he do justice to individual passages that relate to that theme? Nowhere is this relationship more evident than in Ecclesiastes. Leland Ryken does a masterful job of explaining the theme(s) of Ecclesiastes as well as to give us an overview of the content. With respect to the theme he states:

Ecclesiastes presents a major theme and a minor theme. The major theme is the denial of meaning or satisfaction in life considered by itself. What spoils life in the negative passage of Ecclesiastes is the attempt to get more out of life – out of work, pleasure, money, food – than life itself can provide. The minor theme is that meaning can be found in living earthly life as part of a bigger reality governed by the presence of God. The writer thus uses a very common literary strategy: he demonstrates at length the inadequacy of a common worldview and combines with this demonstration an alternate world view. . . . The dialectical structures of contrasts – the alternate sections of despair and affirmation, the futile quest versus its successful conclusion – expresses the double theme of the book.[33]

Understanding these two contrasting themes is absolutely essential if an expositor is going to preach through this difficult book. No book has been misinterpreted and misapplied more than Ecclesiastes. Understanding it properly will give hope and bring balance to a life that is filled with the conflict between good and evil, vexation and fulfillment. Misinterpreting it will cause a believer to become confused and fatalistic about life's outlook. It could encourage him to throw caution to the wind and indulge in the very things that Solomon warned would not bring fulfillment. To properly preach through Ecclesiastes, therefore, is to understand it.

Ryken's outline (I put his exact thoughts in outline form) through the first half of the book will help you grasp the meaning of Ecclesiastes.

I.   Introduction (1:1-3) *introduction to narrator and theme*
II.   Protestations (1:4-2:23)
    1. Of the meaningless cycles of life (1:4-11)
    2. Of the inability to find satisfaction (1:12-23)
        1) In knowledge (1:12-18)
        2) In pleasure and wealth (2:1-11)

---

[33] Ryken, 271.

          3) In permanent achievement (2:12-17)
          4) In work (2:18-23)

III.   Affirmations (2:24-3:22)
      1. Enjoyment as God's gift (2:24-26)
      2. Concerning time (3:1-22)
      3. Viewed from human perspective (3:1-8)
      4. Viewed from the divine perspective (3:9-22)

IV.   Contradistinctions *i.e. comparisons; one balanced against the other* (4:1-7:14)
      1. First set (4:1-12)
          1) Futile quest to find meaning in wealth (4:1-8)
          2) Ideal of human companionship (4:9-12)
      2. Second set (4:13-5:7)
          1) Fickleness of fame (4:13-16)
          2) Picture of the person as a worshiper (5:1-7)
      3. Third set (5:8-20)
          1) Limitations of money (5:8-17)
          2) Life lived with God as the center (5:18-20)
      4. Fourth set (6:1-7:14)
          1) Tragic nature of this life (6, 7:1-8)
          2) Assurance amidst the tragedies of life (7:9-14)[34]

Roman numeral IV, *the Contradistinctions*, depicts alternating ideas that balance each other for the purpose of emphasis. For example, *the futile quest to find meaning in wealth* is balanced with *the ideal of human companionship*. In other words the vain pursuit of wealth,

---

[34] Ryken, *Ecclesiastes,* <u>A Complete Literary Guide to the Bible</u>, 272.

which is what humans typically do, is balanced by the fact that there is something that money can't buy and that is true human companionship. The advantage of having a good outline like this one is that the preacher can organize his sermons around these sections and be assured that he is properly tracing the progression of thought. Each of these sections must be interpreted in light of the book's two themes. We will pick one of these sections and create a sermonic outline from it.

Example: Ecclesiastes 4:13-16

Better is a poor and a wise child than an old and foolish king, who will no more be admonished. 14 For out of prison he cometh to reign; whereas also he that is born in his kingdom becometh poor. 15 I considered all the living which walk under the sun, with the second child that shall stand up in his stead. 16 There is no end of all the people, even of all that have been before them: they also that come after shall not rejoice in him. Surely this also is vanity and vexation of spirit.

Theme   The fickleness of fame: *Pursuing Fame apart from God is Futility*

Type   Exposition/Wisdom/Eccles.

Main Divisions:

I.   Fame is Fickle in Light of its Humble Beginnings (13) *i.e. the qualities of virtue and youthfulness offered hope but it turned out to be irrelevant in the end*

II.   Fame is Fickle in Light of the Struggles Along the Way (14) *i.e. even though the virtuous youth had to overcome great hardships people didn't care in the end*

III.   Fame is Fickle in Light of the Great Success at the Pinnacle of One's Career (15-16) *i.e. in spite of a great following and success things always change and it didn't matter in the end*

BIBLICAL EXPOSITION FROM THE PSALM GENRE

The genre of Psalms consists of the book of Psalms, the Song of Solomon, and Lamentations. Each of these books possesses their own challenges regarding creating sermonic outlines. We will look at each book and their unique characteristics as we learn how to preach from them.

Psalms

One of the difficulties concerning the book of Psalms is the attempt to classify them into logical categories. One method has been to group them either by virtue of content or function. Classifying all the Psalms into only two categories, however, does not seem to do justice to their diversity. Using content and function as a base, C. Hassell Bullock divides all 150 Psalms into six categories: Hymns, penitential Psalms, wisdom Psalms, messianic Psalms, imprecatory Psalms, and "enthronement" Psalms.[35] He qualifies this list, however, with the understanding that his list is "by no means exhaustive." These six categories will have to do for us. I will not attempt to outline an example from each category because the principles of *Thematic Preaching* remain the same.

Hymns

Hymn Psalms are divided into two sub categories: Hymns of praise and hymns of Zion, each stressing their respective content. They are called "hymns" because they were sung on holy days in the temple. Bullock lists the following Psalms as hymns: 8, 19, 29, 33, 65, 67, 100, 103,

---

[35] C. Hassell Bullock, An Introduction to the Old Testament Poetic Books (Chicago: Moody Press, 1988), 135-142.

104, 105, 111, 113, 114, 135, 136, 145, 146, 147, 148, 149, 150, 46, 48, 76, 84, 87, 122, 47, 93, 96, 97, 98, 99.[36]

Example: Psalm 100

Make a joyful shout to the Lord, all you lands! 2 Serve the Lord with gladness; Come before His presence with singing. 3 Know that the Lord, He is God; It is He who has made us, and not we ourselves; We are His people and the sheep of His pasture. 4 Enter into His gates with thanksgiving, and into His courts with praise. Be thankful to Him, and bless His name. 5 For the Lord is good; His mercy is everlasting, His truth endures to all generations. (NKJV)

Theme   Admonition to praise God joyfully
Type   Exposition/Psalm Genre/Psalm
Main Divisions:

    I.   Mandate to Praise God joyously (1-2)
          1. The scope of the mandate *"all you lands"*
          2. The style of the mandate
              1) Loudly *"shout"*
              2) Gladly *"gladness"*
              3) Melodiously *"singing"*
    II.   Motivation to Praise God joyously (3)
          1. Who God is with respect to Himself
              1) Yahweh (LORD)
              2) Elohim (God)
           2. Who God is with respect to us
              1) Creator
                  (1) We are his people
                  (2) We are the sheep of His pasture
              2) Sustainer: *"and not we ourselves"*
    III.   Mandate to Praise God joyously (4)
          1. Mandated to give thanks

---

[36] Bullock, 135.

2. Mandated to give praise
IV. Motivation to Praise God joyously (5)
   1. Motivated because of His goodness
   2. Motivated because of His mercy
   3. Motivated because of His truth
   4. Motivated because of His eternality

Willem A. VanGemeren in his commentary on Psalms gives a very similar analysis of Psalm 100. [37]

A Call to give thanks (vv. 1-2)
      B Celebration of the covenant (v. 3)
A' Call to give thanks (v. 4)
      B' Celebration of the covenant (v. 5)

Notice that my division *The Mandate to Praise God* corresponds to his division *Call to give thanks.* These say the same thing. Furthermore, my other division *Motivation to Praise God* corresponds to his *Celebration of the covenant.* Our motivation to praise God is who He is and what He has done. In Old Testament language that speaks of a covenant relationship.

Penitential Psalms

The penitential Psalms are 6, 32, 38, 51, 102, 130, and 143. These depict the writer as mourning and repenting for his sin. Some of them (e.g. 38 and 51) portray a saint who has committed a serious transgression of the Law and express genuine remorse for his actions. Others are not quite as demonstrative about their past failings but confess their sin in general.

---

[37]Willem A. VanGemeren, *Psalms,* The Expositor's Bible Commentary, vol. 5, ed. Frank E. Gaebelein, (Grand Rapids: Zondervan Pub. House, 1991), 638.

Example: Ps. 6

O Lord, rebuke me not in thine anger, neither chasten me in thy hot displeasure. 2 Have mercy upon me, O Lord; for I am weak: O Lord, heal me; for my bones are vexed. 3 My soul is also sore vexed: but thou, O Lord, how long? 4 Return, O Lord, deliver my soul: oh save me for thy mercies' sake. 5 For in death there is no remembrance of thee: in the grave who shall give thee thanks? 6 I am weary with my groaning; all the night make I my bed to swim; I water my couch with my tears. 7 Mine eye is consumed because of grief; it waxeth old because of all mine enemies. 8 Depart from me, all ye workers of iniquity; for the Lord hath heard the voice of my weeping. 9 The Lord hath heard my supplication; the Lord will receive my prayer. 10 Let all mine enemies be ashamed and sore vexed: let them return and be ashamed suddenly.

Theme   Prayer of the Penitent
Type   Exposition/Psalm Genre/Psalm
Main Divisions:

   I.   The Plea of the Penitent (1-5)
      1. A plea for kindness (1)
         1) Don't rebuke
         2) Don't chasten in hot displeasure
      2. A plea for mercy (2a)
         1) The record of the plea *"Have mercy on me, O LORD"*
         2) The reason for the plea *"for I am weak"*
      3. A plea for healing (2b-3)
         1) The record of the plea *"Oh LORD, heal me"*
         2) The reasons for the plea
            (1) "for my bones are vexed"
            (2) "My soul is also is sore vexed"
      4. A plea for deliverance (4-5)
         1) The record of the plea (4a) *"O LORD, deliver me!"*

       2) The rationale for the plea (4b) *"Oh, save me for thy mercy's sake!"*

       3) The reasons for the plea (5)

          (3) Dead people do not remember God

          (4) Dead people do not give God thanks

II.   The Plight of the Penitent (6-7)

    1. He groans (6a) *"I am weary with my groaning"*

    2. He cries (6b)

       1) *"all night I make my bed swim"*

       2) *"I water my couch with my tears"*

    3. He grows weary (7)

       1) *"Mine eye is consumed because of grief'*

       2) *"it waxeth old because of all mine enemies"*

III.   The Praise of the Penitent (8-10)

    1. The command in the praise (8) *"Depart from me, all ye workers of iniquity"*

    2. The confidence of the praise (9) *"The LORD hath heard . . . The LORD will receive"*

    3. The condemnation in the praise (10)

       1) *"enemies be ashamed"*

       2) *"greatly troubled"*

       3) *"turn back suddenly"*

Enthronement Psalms

The enthronement Psalms are 47, 93, and 95-99. While the theme and content of these Psalms deal with God being enthroned as King of heaven and earth their structure is not much different than those of the hymns.

Example: Psalm 47

Oh, clap your hands, all you peoples! Shout to God with the voice of triumph! 2 For the Lord Most High is awesome; He is a great King over all the earth. 3 He will subdue the peoples under us, And the nations under our feet. 4 He will choose our inheritance for us, The excellence of Jacob whom He loves. Selah 5 God has gone up with a shout, The Lord with the sound of a trumpet. 6 Sing praises to God, sing praises! Sing praises to our King, sing praises! 7 For God is the King of all the earth; Sing praises with understanding. 8 God reigns over the nations; God sits on His holy throne. 9 The princes of the people have gathered together, The people of the God of Abraham. For the shields of the earth belong to God; He is greatly exalted. (NKJV)

Theme   The Mandate to Joyfully Praise the King of
               the Earth
Type   Exposition/Psalm Genre/Psalm
Main Divisions:

I.   Mandated Because of His Kingly Relationship
        (1-4)
        1. The mandate expressed (1)
           1) *"Clap your hands"*
           2) *"Shout unto God"*
        2. The mandate expounded (2-4)
           1) His description warrants this
              relationship (2)
              (1) *"Lord Most High is awesome"*
              (2) *"He is a great King over all the
                  earth"*
           2) His deeds betoken this relationship (3-4)
              (1) *"He will subdue the peoples under us
                  and the nations under our feet"* (3)
              (2) *"He will choose our inheritance for
                  us, The excellence of Jacob whom He
                  loves"* (4)
II.   Mandated Because of His Kingly Right (5-7)
        1. The expression on account of His right (5)
           *"God has gone up with a shout, The Lord with the
           sound of a trumpet"*

2. The exaltation on account of His right (6-7)
"Sing praises to our King, sing praises!"
III. Mandated Because of His Kingly Reign (8-9)
1. His manifold people
1) *"the nations" (8a)*
2) *"The princes of the people" (9a)*
3) *"The people of the God of Abraham"* (9b)
2. His majestic place (8b) *"His holy throne"*
3. His magnificent position (9c) *"He is greatly exalted"*

There are a few things to take notice with this Psalm. First, it was very difficult to create distinct main divisions because the sentiments throughout were repetitious and intertwined. It is necessary in such cases to take a step back and look at it from several different standpoints. I eventually noticed that in spite of the repetition there were slight differences in subject matter present in three different sections of the Psalm. All three sections had the overriding theme of the King of the earth being praised but each section portrayed a slightly different aspect of it. The first emphasized the covenant motif of the people of Israel. The second portrays God actively involved in the process asserting His rights as King. The last demonstrates his Kingly rule or reign. As I stated earlier the Psalms are among the most difficult passages of Scripture to put in outline form.

Messianic

Example: Psalm 18 (Taken from 2 Sam. 22)

Please refer to 2 Samuel 22 so and then return here in order to examine the outline for yourself.

Theme   Adoration and Rejoicing for God's
Deliverance

Type   Exposition/Psalm Genre/Psalm

Main Divisions:

I.   The Praise for Deliverance (1-4)
      1. Metaphors of praise (2-3)
      2. Motivation for praise (4)

II.   The Petition for Deliverance (5-7)
      1. Circumstances of his petition (5-6)
      2. Certainty of his petition (7)

III.   The Power of Deliverance (8-20)
      1. Powerfully represented (8-16): Theophany
      2. Powerfully rescued (17-20)

IV.   The Principle of his Deliverance (21-30)
      1. The example of this principle: David (21-25)
      2. The elaboration of this principle (26-30)

V.   The Provenance (source) for Deliverance (31-37)

VI.   The Punishment in Deliverance (38-46)

VII. The Praise for Deliverance (47-51)
      1. Praise for Yahweh (47-49)
         1) Because he avenges (48)
         2) Because he exalts (49)
      2. Praise for Yahweh (50-51)
         1) Because he give victories
         2) Because he shows kindness

This Psalm is recorded both in Psalm 18 as well as 2 Samuel 22 (where this was taken from) with very slight variations. The reader should turn to 2 Samuel and follow along. The writer of 2 Samuel wanted to include it because it was a fitting capstone of David's deliverance from his long struggle with his enemies.

Song of Solomon

The Song of Solomon (or, Song of Songs, Canticles) is unique among Scripture in that the entire book consists of direct discourse between its two main characters, Solomon and the Shulamite. This presents its own challenges by way of organizing its sections into outline form. As with all books of the Bible understanding the Song of Solomon's overall theme and literary organization is key to understanding its parts. Dennis F. Kinlaw divides the book into logical sections as follows:

I.   The Title (1:1)
II.   Courtship (1:2-3:5)
III. The Bridal Procession (3:6-11)
IV.   The Wedding (4:1-5:1)
V.   The Life of Love (5:2-8:7)
VI.   Conclusion (8:8-14)[38]

Obviously the theme of the entire book pertains to the love relationship between two people. The logical manner of organization of the outline above traces the couple's romance from start to finish. It will serve as a good outline of the book of the Song of Solomon. We will examine a few sections of this direct discourse and apply *Thematic Preaching* to it.

Example: Song of Solomon 3:1-5

The Shulamite

By night on my bed I sought the one I love; I sought him, but I did not find him. 2 "I will rise now," I said, "And go about the city; in the

---

[38] Dennis F. Kinlaw, *Song of Songs,* The Expositor's Bible Commentary, Vol. 5, ed. Frank E. Gaebelein (Grand Rapids: Zondervan Pub. House, 1993), 1214.

streets and in the squares I will seek the one I love." I sought him, but I did not find him. 3 The watchmen who go about the city found me; I said, "Have you seen the one I love?" 4 Scarcely had I passed by them, When I found the one I love. I held him and would not let him go, until I had brought him to the house of my mother, And into the chamber of her who conceived me. 5 I charge you, O daughters of Jerusalem, By the gazelles or by the does of the field, Do not stir up nor awaken love Until it pleases. (NKJV)

Theme A Lover Seeking Her Love
Type Exposition/Psalm Genre/Song of Solomon-
Direct Discourse

Main Divisions:

I. The Circumstances of Her Search (1)
    1. It was midnight
    2. He was missing
II. The Course of Her Search (2) *"about the city," "In the streets," "in the squares"*
III. The Companions of Her Search (3) *"The watchmen"*
IV. The Completion of Her Search (4) *"I found the one I love"*
V. The Counsel After Her Search (5) *"I charge you, O daughters of Jerusalem . . . "*

The context of this particular passage is from the larger section depicting the courtship motif. The text concludes the courtship with hints of the coming honeymoon. There are numerous applications the expositor can make. He can stress the practical aspect in order to encourage the audience back to the passion and purity of their early days of romance or he can use it figuratively in the sense that believers should seek Christ with the intensity of the Shulamite. Perhaps he can do both. In either case he must

199

spiritualize the verses to give the passage the fullest possible application for daily living.

Example: Song of Solomon 3:6-11

The Shulamite

Who is this coming out of the wilderness like pillars of smoke, perfumed with myrrh and frankincense, with all the merchant's fragrant powders? 7 Behold, it is Solomon's couch, with sixty valiant men around it, of the valiant of Israel. 8 They all hold swords, being expert in war. Every man has his sword on his thigh because of fear in the night. 9 Of the wood of Lebanon Solomon the King made himself a palanquin: 10 He made its pillars of silver, its support of gold, its seat of purple, its interior paved with love by the daughters of Jerusalem. 11 Go forth, O daughters of Zion, and see King Solomon with the crown with which his mother crowned him on the day of his wedding, the day of the gladness of his heart. (NKJV)

Theme	The Shulamite Rejoices at Solomon's Procession: *The King is Coming!*
Type	Exposition/Psalm Genre/Direct Discourse

Main Divisions:

I. His perfume (6)
II. His platoon (7-8)
1. His platoon is amassed *"sixty valiant men"*
2. His platoon is armed *"Every man has his sword on his thigh"*
3. His platoon is accomplished *"expert in war"*
III. His palanquin (9-10) *i.e. cart on which Solomon was brought in*
IV. His praise (11) *"Go forth, O daughters of Zion, and see King Solomon"*

Now that we have an outline of Solomon's procession, how can we adapt this for our congregations today? Here is one possibility.

I.   His Perfume (6)

Eph. 5:2 "And walk in love, as Christ also has loved us and given Himself for us, an offering and a sacrifice to God for a sweet-smelling aroma"

II.   His Platoon (7-8)

Rev. 19:11 "And the armies which were in heaven followed him upon white horses, clothed in fine linen, white and clean."

III. His Palanquin (9-10)

Rev. 19:11 "And I saw heaven opened, and behold a white horse; and he that sat upon him was called Faithful and True"

IV.   His Praise (11)

Romans 14:11 "For it is written, As I live, saith the Lord, every knee shall bow to me, and every tongue shall confess to God."

Lamentations

Lamentations is the final book of the psalm genre and bears many marks of a psalm of lament. Chapter 5 contains 22 verses, the normal length of a Hebrew poem as do chapters 1, 2, and 4. Chapters 1-4 are built on an alphabetical acrostic much like Psalm 119 with each of the 22 verses beginning with a successive letter in the Hebrew alphabet. Chapter 3, the exception, has 66 verses and every three verses begin with a successive letter of the Hebrew alphabet. Clearly the book of Lamentations is a poem of lament.

Merrill Unger divides Lamentations into five sections noticeable in the outline below. This five-fold division seems to be the consensus of opinion regarding the logical organization of the book.

I.   Lament over desolated Jerusalem (1:1-22)

II.   The Lord's judgment and its purpose (2:1-22)

III.   The prophet's lament and hope (3:1-66)
IV.   The prophet's account of Jerusalem's fall (4:1-22)
V.   The prophet's prayer for mercy (5:1-22)[39]

Example: Lamentations 4:12-16

The kings of the earth, and all the inhabitants of the world, would not have believed that the adversary and the enemy should have entered into the gates of Jerusalem. 13 For the sins of her prophets, and the iniquities of her priests, that have shed the blood of the just in the midst of her, 14 They have wandered as blind men in the streets, they have polluted themselves with blood, so that men could not touch their garments. 15 They cried unto them, Depart ye; it is unclean; depart, depart, touch not: when they fled away and wandered, they said among the heathen, They shall no more sojourn there. 16 The anger of the Lord hath divided them; he will no more regard them: they respected not the persons of the priests, they favoured not the elders.

Theme   The Cause for the Destruction of Jerusalem
Type   Exposition/Psalm Genre/Lamentations
Main Divisions:

I.   Consternation at the Destruction of Jerusalem (12)
II.   Provocation for the Destruction of Jerusalem (13-16)
    1. The guilty parties identified (13a)
    2. The guilty parties indicted (13b-16)
        1) They are discolored with blood (13b)
        2) They are defiled with blame (14-16)
            (1) The reclusiveness b/c of their defilement (14a)

---

[39] Merrill F. Unger, <u>Unger's Commentary on the Old Testament</u>, Vol. II (Chicago: Moody Press, 1981), 1473.

(2) The recognition of their defilement
(14b-15)
1. They know it (14b-15b)
   1) They were treated as lepers
      (14b, c)
   2) They behaved as lepers
      (15a, b)
2. Others know it (15c, d)
(3) The regard for their defilement (16)
1. The Lord does not regard them
   (16a)
2. The people do not regard them
   (16b)

PROPHESY GENRE

The prophesy genre consists of all the major and minor prophets of the Old Testament. (Daniel, classified as apocalyptic, is not included.) This larger classification is replete with numerous smaller categories of genre.

Dr. Richard Patterson cites the following genres common in prophetic literature: Prayer (especially in Jeremiah), hymns and songs, laments, Hebrew epic, and satire (Amos and Jonah may be viewed essentially as satire) which often utilizes metaphor, simile, and irony in biting criticism against the sin of the recipients.[40] While most of the individual genres are handled in similar fashion to those already discussed some of them deserve mention. Notice what Leland Ryken says about Amos 4:1-2:

---

[40] Richard Patterson, *Old Testament Prophesy*, <u>A Complete Literary Guide to the Bible</u> eds. Leland Ryken and Tremper Longman (Grand Rapids: Zondervan Pub. House, 1988), 305-306.

The vehicle here is direct vituperation (violent denunciation), beginning with a denigrating metaphor that compares wealthy women to cows (Bashan was a grain producing region capable of producing fat livestock). The specific objects of attack are an affluent and self-indulgent lifestyle coupled with indifference to the suffering of the poverty-stricken. The scornful invective merges with the prophetic formula of predicting woe for the guilty, with the prediction itself becoming part of the attack. Again, it is the character of God (specifically his holiness) that provides the norm by which the satire is conducted, and the tone is biting.[41]

Example: Amos 4:1-2

Hear this word, ye kine of Bashan, that are in the mountain of Samaria, which oppress the poor, which crush the needy, which say to their masters, Bring, and let us drink. 2 The Lord God hath sworn by his holiness, that, lo, the days shall come upon you, that he will take you away with hooks, and your posterity with fishhooks.

Theme   Pronunciation of judgment against the indifferent wealthy Israelites

Type   Exposition/Prophesy/Satire

Main Divisions:

   I.   Their Comparison (1a): *Wealthy women compared to fat cows*

   II.   Their Crime (1b)

   III.   Their Condemnation (2)

       1. The solemnness of the condemnation (2a) *"sworn by His holiness"*

       2. The sentence of the condemnation (2b) *"take you away with fishhooks"*

This outline follows the same manner of breaking the passage up into its component parts as the other genres we have already discussed. The flexibility of *Thematic*

---

[41] Ryken, *Amos*, <u>A Complete Literary Guide to the Bible</u>, 341.

Preaching allows it to conform to the specific nature of each individual genre.

Amos uses the subgenre of proverb very effectively in his satire on the sinning people of Israel. Sometimes entire passages consist of a string of parallel proverbs in order to make a point. The question is, what does a preacher do when he is faced with a string of proverbs such as those found in Amos 3:3-6? Is there enough of a message to feed his congregation? The expositor must decide whether he wants to use such a passage as the whole basis for his message or combine other verses with it in order to expand the theme. The verses below all ask rhetorical questions and arrive at the same conclusion. The Lord is, in fact, responsible for the future calamity on sinning Israel.

Example: Amos 3:3-6

3 Can two walk together, unless they are agreed? 4 Will a lion roar in the forest, when he has no prey? Will a young lion cry out of his den, if he has caught nothing? 5 Will a bird fall into a snare on the earth, where there is no trap for it? Will a snare spring up from the earth, if it has caught nothing at all? 6 If a trumpet is blown in a city, will not the people be afraid? If there is calamity in a city, will not the Lord have done it? (NKJV)

Theme   Questions indicating the certainty of the coming calamity

Type   Exposition/Prophesy/Satire/Proverb

Main Divisions:

     I.   The Questions are Copious *(i.e. The Lord asks 7 rhetorical questions to drive His point home. Much like Joseph's dream in which it was repeated twice for certainty)*

     II.   The Questions are Common *(i.e. The vivid and common nature of the questions aid the hearer in understanding the obvious answer. This is where each unique question can be analyzed according to its own nature and discussed)*

III.   The Questions are Critical *(i.e. The answer to them is very serious. The Lord will bring judgment on the Israelites!)*

The book of Zephaniah contains at least three subgenres according to Dr. Richard Patterson: Announcement of judgments, Kingdom oracles, and instructional accounts.[42] In addition these subgenres also contain elements of apocalyptic and hymn. Using Zephaniah 3:1-7 as our next example Dr. Patterson breaks this passage up into three distinct sections: Invective (1), criticism (2-4), and threat (5-7).[43] Let's take a look at a complete outline.

Example: Zephaniah 3:1-7

Woe to her that is filthy and polluted, to the oppressing city! 2 She obeyed not the voice; she received not correction; she trusted not in the Lord; she drew not near to her God. 3 Her princes within her are roaring lions; her judges are evening wolves; they gnaw not the bones till the morrow. 4 Her prophets are light and treacherous persons: her priests have polluted the sanctuary, they have done violence to the law. 5 The just Lord is in the midst thereof; he will not do iniquity: every morning doth he bring his judgment to light, he faileth not; but the unjust knoweth no shame. 6 I have cut off the nations: their towers are desolate; I made their streets waste, that none passeth by: their cities are destroyed, so that there is no man, that there is none inhabitant. 7 I said, Surely thou wilt fear me, thou wilt receive instruction; so their dwelling should not be cut off, howsoever I punished them: but they rose early, and corrupted all their doings.

Theme   The Danger of Jerusalem's Imminent Judgment

---

[42] Patterson, 300-304.
[43] Ibid., 301.

Type   Exposition/Prophesy/Judgment
Main Divisions:

I.   Jerusalem's Woe (1) *i.e. invective*
II.   Jerusalem's Waywardness (2-4) *i.e. criticism*
        1. Her crimes (2)
            1) Disobedience
            2) Incorrigibility
            3) Faithlessness
            4) Avoidance
        2. Her commanders (3-4)
            1) Princes are lions
            2) Judges are wolves
            3) Prophets are insolent and treacherous
            4) Priests are polluting and violent
III.   Jerusalem's Warning (5-7) *i.e. threat*
        1. The source of the warning (5-6): The Lord
            1) His attributes (5)
                (1) Righteousness
                (2) Justice
            2) His annihilation (6)
                (1) Of nations
                (2) Of fortresses
                (3) Of cities & streets
        2. The supposition about the warning (7)
            1) The supposition stated (7ab)
            2) The supposition scorned (7c)

APOCALYPTIC GENRE

The only two books in the Bible that are classified as apocalyptic are Daniel and Revelation. Some other books, particularly among the prophets, have sections that are apocalyptic but only Daniel and Revelation are classified as such in their entirety. Among other features apocalyptic literature contains a large amount of epic combined with imagery and symbolism. We previously outlined Revelation 12 using literary analysis as the primary tool but now we will apply the typical method of *Thematic Preaching* and see what we come up with.

One of the greatest Bible expositors and Christian leaders of our day is Dr. John MacArthur Jr. Besides his successful radio broadcast "Grace to You," his many years of pastoring a mega-church in California, and his being president of the Master's College, Dr. MacArthur has authored over 80 books, the majority of which are commentaries on the Bible. I highly recommend his commentaries not only because he successfully balances scholarship with practical application but because his manner of outlining follows *Thematic Preaching* to the "T." Notice the following three examples taken from his first volume on Revelation:

Example: Rev. 5:1-14

Theme   A Vision of the Lamb-The Worthy one
Type   Exposition/Apocalyptic
Main Divisions:

    I.   The Search for the Worthy One (5:2-4)
    II.   The Selection of the Worthy One (5:5-7)
    III.   The Song of the Worthy One (5:8-14)[44]

Example: Rev. 6:12-17

---

[44] John F. MacArthur Jr., *The Book of Revelation*, The MacArthur New Testament Commentary, vol. 1 (Chicago: Moody Press, 1999), 161.

And I beheld when he had opened the sixth seal, and, lo, there was a great earthquake; and the sun became black as sackcloth of hair, and the moon became as blood; 13 And the stars of heaven fell unto the earth, even as a fig tree casteth her untimely figs, when she is shaken of a mighty wind. 14 And the heaven departed as a scroll when it is rolled together; and every mountain and island were moved out of their places. 15 And the kings of the earth, and the great men, and the rich men, and the chief captains, and the mighty men, and every bondman, and every free man, hid themselves in the dens and in the rocks of the mountains; 16 And said to the mountains and rocks, Fall on us, and hide us from the face of him that sitteth on the throne, and from the wrath of the Lamb: 17 For the great day of his wrath is come; and who shall be able to stand?

Theme   Fear of the Wrath to Come: The 6th Seal

Type   Exposition/Apocalyptic

Main Divisions:

    I.   The Reason for the Fear (12-14)

    II.   The Range of the Fear (15a)

    III.   The Reaction of Fear (15b-17)[45]

Example: Rev. 8:1-5

And when he had opened the seventh seal, there was silence in heaven about the space of half an hour. 2 And I saw the seven angels which stood before God; and to them were given seven trumpets. 3 And another angel came and stood at the altar, having a golden censer; and there was given unto him much incense, that he should offer it with the prayers of all saints upon the golden altar which was before the throne. 4 And the smoke of the incense, which came with the prayers of the saints, ascended up before God out of the angel's hand. 5 And the angel took the censer, and filled it with fire of the altar, and cast it into the earth: and there were voices, and thunderings, and lightnings, and an earthquake.

---

[45] MacArthur, 199.

Theme	The Seventh Seal
Type	Exposition/Apocalyptic
Main Divisions:	

I.   The Silence at the Seventh seal (8:1)
II.   The Sounding of the Seventh seal (8:2)
III. The Supplication of the Seventh seal (8:3-4)
IV.   The Storm of the Seventh Seal (8:5)[46]

MacArthur treats apocalyptic genre in the same manner as the other genres. There are peculiarities with each but their manner of treatment is very similar. This is because *Thematic Preaching's* system of outlining expository messages is extremely accommodating and flexible. The next example taken from Daniel 7 is an example of apocalyptic literature from the Old Testament. As the reader will see I handle this in similar fashion that MacArthur handles the passages from Revelation.

Example: Dan. 7:1-8

In the first year of Belshazzar king of Babylon Daniel had a dream and visions of his head upon his bed: then he wrote the dream, and told the sum of the matters. 2 Daniel spake and said, I saw in my vision by night, and, behold, the four winds of the heaven strove upon the great sea. 3 And four great beasts came up from the sea, diverse one from another. 4 The first was like a lion, and had eagle's wings: I beheld till the wings thereof were plucked, and it was lifted up from the earth, and made stand upon the feet as a man, and a man's heart was given to it. 5 And behold another beast, a second, like to a bear, and it raised up itself on one side, and it had three ribs in the mouth of it between the teeth of it: and they said thus unto it, Arise, devour much flesh. 6 After this I beheld, and lo another, like a leopard, which had upon the back of it four wings of a fowl; the beast had also four heads; and dominion was given to it. 7 After this I saw in the night visions, and

---

[46] MacArthur, 235.

behold a fourth beast, dreadful and terrible, and strong exceedingly;
and it had great iron teeth: it devoured and brake in pieces, and
stamped the residue with the feet of it: and it was diverse from all the
beasts that were before it; and it had ten horns. 8 I considered the
horns, and, behold, there came up among them another little horn,
before whom there were three of the first horns plucked up by the
roots: and, behold, in this horn were eyes like the eyes of man, and a
mouth speaking great things.

Theme   Daniel's Vision of the Four Beasts
Type   Exposition/Apocalyptic
Main Divisions:

I.   The Circumstances of the Vision of the Four
       Beasts (1ab)
       1. The time of the vision (1a)
       2. The type of vision: *a dream while sleeping on his*
           bed (1b)
II.   The Chronicle of the Vision of the Four Beasts
       (1c-8)
       1. The source of the four beasts *"stirring up the*
           Great Sea" i.e. the tumultuous Gentile world (2, 3a)
       2. The sketch of the four beasts
           (1) The distinctiveness of the four beasts
               (3b)
           (2) The details of the four beasts (4-8)
               1) Lion w/eagles wings i.e.
                   Nebuchadnezzar/Babylon (4)
                   1. His humiliation (4b)
                   2. His humanization (4cd)
               2) Bear i.e. Medo-Persia (5)
                   1. His awkwardness (5b)
                   2. His appetite (5c)
                   3. His aggressiveness (5d)
               3) Leopard i.e. Greece (6)

        1. His dynamics (6bc)
          1) Four heads
          2) Four wings
        2. His dominion (6d)
    4) Fourth Beast (7-8)
        1. His characteristics (7ab)
          1) Fearful
          2) Formidable
        2. His canines (7c)
        3. His carnage (7d) "devouring, breaking in pieces, and trampling"
        4. His contrasts (7e,f)
          1) His anomaly (7e) "It was different from all the beasts"
          2) His antlers (7f-8)
            (1) Their number i.e. 10 (7f)
            (2) Their nemesis i.e. the little horn (8)
              1. His conquest
              2. His characteristics
                1) He is human
                2) He is haughty

GOSPEL GENRE

The Gospel genre consisting of Matthew, Mark, Luke, and John is mainly comprised of alternating sections of narrative and discourse. The synoptics contain elements of prophesy as well and John is unique in that it has very large portions of continuous direct discourse between Jesus and his adversaries. We have already outlined passages from these genres but there are a few subgenres the Gospels contain that we haven't outlined yet (even though they may be found in the other major genres as well): Sermon, prayer, and parable.

In one respect we have already dealt with prayer in that the psalms are songs of prayer to God. Certainly prayer can be found in many of the Old Testament books such as Hannah's prayer, Moses' prayer, Abraham's servant's prayer, etc. The denunciations of the prophets may be compared to sermons in that they are proclamations of God's Word to the people. Parable, on the other hand, is unique to the Gospels. Perhaps some scholars could present a good case as to why other portions of Scripture should be considered parable also yet no other sections of Scripture contains the volume and consistency of the parables as those found in the Gospels. For the sake of thoroughness we will begin by outlining the model prayer.

Prayer

Example: Matt. 6:9-13

In this manner, therefore, pray: Our Father in heaven, hallowed be Your name. 10 Your kingdom come. Your will be done on earth as it is in heaven. 11 Give us this day our daily bread. 12 And forgive us our debts, as we forgive our debtors. 13 And do not lead us into temptation, but deliver us from the evil one. For Yours is the kingdom and the power and the glory forever. Amen. (NKJV)

Theme   Four Elements of the Model Prayer
Type   Exposition/Gospel/Prayer
Main Divisions:

    I.   Recognition (9)
           1. We recognize His relationship (9b) *"Our Father in heaven"*
           2. We recognize His reverence (9c) *"hallowed be Your name"*

II.	Submission (10)
   1.	A total submission (10a, b)
      (1)	We submit to His domain
      (2)	We submit to His decisions
   2.	A terrestrial submission *"on earth as it is in heaven"* (10c)
III.	Petition (11-13b)
   1.	A petition for provision (11)
   2.	A petition for pardon (12)
   3.	A petition for preservation (13a, b)
IV.	Glorification (13c)
   1.	We glorify Him b/c of His majesty
   2.	We glorify Him b/c of His might
   3.	We glorify Him b/c of His magnificence

Direct Discourse

Example: John 8:48-59

Then answered the Jews, and said unto him, Say we not well that thou art a Samaritan, and hast a devil? 49 Jesus answered, I have not a devil; but I honour my Father, and ye do dishonour me. 50 And I seek not mine own glory: there is one that seeketh and judgeth. 51 Verily, verily, I say unto you, If a man keep my saying, he shall never see death. 52 Then said the Jews unto him, Now we know that thou hast a devil. Abraham is dead, and the prophets; and thou sayest, If a man keep my saying, he shall never taste of death. 53 Art thou greater than our father Abraham, which is dead? and the prophets are dead: whom makest thou thyself? 54 Jesus answered, If I honour myself, my honour is nothing: it is my Father that honoureth me; of whom ye say, that he is your God: 55 Yet ye have not known him; but I know him: and if I should say, I know him not, I shall be a liar like unto you: but I know him, and keep his saying. 56 Your father Abraham rejoiced to see my day: and he saw it, and was glad. 57 Then said the Jews unto him, Thou art not yet fifty years old, and hast thou seen Abraham? 58 Jesus said unto them, Verily, verily, I say unto you, Before Abraham was, I am. *59 Then took they up stones to cast at him: but Jesus hid himself, and went out of the temple, going through the midst of them, and so passed by.*

Theme   Jewish Hatred Amid Christ's Claims to Deity
Type   Exposition/Gospel/Indirect Discourse
Main Divisions:

   I.   Their Blasphemy (48-51)
         1. The record of their blasphemy (48)
         2. The rebuttal to their blasphemy (49-51)
             1) Rebutted by virtue of Jesus' humble motivation (49-50)
             2) Rebutted by virtue of Jesus' hopeful declaration (51)
  II.   Their Blunder (52-56)
         1. Their blunder characterized (52-53)
             1) Their blunder is defamatory (52ab)
             2) Their blunder is defective (52c-53)
                i.e. *Defective understanding of eternal life*
         2. Their blunder confuted (54-56)
             1) The source of Christ's recognition confutes it (54)
             2) The sacredness of Christ's relationship confutes it (55-56)
                1. An intimate relationship (55)
                   (1) He knows His father
                   (2) He obeys His father
                2. An immortal relationship (56)
 III.   Their Brutality (57-59)
         1. The reason for their brutality (57-58)
             1) The angry question (57)
             2) The appropriate answer (58)
         2. The reaction of their brutality (59)

The difficulty of outlining passages of direct discourse is due to the conversation shifting from one person to the next. Whose thoughts are the driving force of the text that would determine the main idea? This poses a challenge for the expositor when deciding upon his theme. Should the central motif be Jesus' claims or the angry Jewish response? After spending time analyzing this text I decided that John 8:48-59 stressed the Jewish opposition a little more than Jesus' assertions to deity. It does not mean that their hateful response is more important than Christ's reply. It only means that the passage stresses their angry opposition a little more than it does Christ making his claims. Actually both motifs are involved as my theme portrays. Their rejection of his words causes Him to make His claims which in turn rouse their anger even more. Once it is decided whose actions determine the central motif we use a pronoun to introduce each main division. As the outline above portrays I use the pronoun "their" because the Jewish opposition takes the center stage of this section of John 8.

Not only is finding the right theme tricky because of the dialogue but creating the main divisions is a problem for the same reason. It is not clear where one division starts and another ends. Obviously it would not make sense to begin a new division in the middle of someone's statements but rather at the end. One solution to the problem is to organize the main divisions directly around the gist of each speaker's sentences. This will not always solve the problem, however. I think it is best to take a step back and look at it from a bird's point of view instead of being distracted by the argumentation.

In other words instead of concentrating on each party's particular points concentrate instead on the overall issue. The issue is that the unbelieving Jews are livid at Christ's claims to divinity. Each main division may include statements from both parties. The dialogue is broken up according to the change of subject matter of that entire conversation. The fact that it is direct discourse, therefore, does not alter the method of organizing the outline very much. What is important is that the expositor notices the shift in the subject matter and outlines his sermon accordingly.

If the reader traces the above outline he will find that the divisions make sense and logically portray the contents of the passage. An expositor who is still a novice should not attempt to get too fancy with his outline. The most important thing is that the divisions remain parallel and that they accurately describe the content of the passage. Ultimately the thing that matters most is that the congregation can easily follow the expositor's train of thought.

One of the drawbacks of expository preaching is that the sermon can be reduced to a running commentary with no relevant substance or application. A safeguard against this tendency is to keep the language of the outline as simple as possible. When a sermon contains a simply-stated theme along with simply-stated main divisions the message has a much greater tendency to be purposeful. The simpler the language the easier it is for the audience to make the spiritual connections. Alliteration is helpful because it tends to reduce the amount of necessary words. In addition, it makes it easier for the audience to remember the expositor's main points.

Parable

Example: Matt. 13:24-30, 36-43

24 Another parable He put forth to them, saying: "The kingdom of heaven is like a man who sowed good seed in his field; 25 but while men slept, his enemy came and sowed tares among the wheat and went his way. 26 But when the grain had sprouted and produced a crop, then the tares also appeared. 27 So the servants of the owner came and said to him, 'Sir, did you not sow good seed in your field? How then does it have tares?' 28 He said to them, 'An enemy has done this.' The servants said to him, 'Do you want us then to go and gather them up?' 29 But he said, 'No, lest while you gather up the tares you also uproot the wheat with them. 30 Let both grow together until the harvest, and at the time of harvest I will say to the reapers, "First gather together the tares and bind them in bundles to burn them, but gather the wheat into my barn."'"36 Then Jesus sent the multitude away and went into the house. And His disciples came to Him, saying, "Explain to us the parable of the tares of the field." 37 He answered and said to them: "He who sows the good seed is the Son of Man. 38 The field is the world, the good seeds are the sons of the kingdom, but the tares are the sons of the wicked one. 39 The enemy who sowed them is the devil, the harvest is the end of the age, and the reapers are the angels. 40 Therefore as the tares are gathered and burned in the fire, so it will be at the end of this age. 41 The Son of Man will send out His angels, and they will gather out of His kingdom all things that offend, and those who practice lawlessness, 42 and will cast them into the furnace of fire. There will be wailing and gnashing of teeth. 43 Then the righteous will shine forth as the sun in the kingdom of their Father. He who has ears to hear, let him hear! (NKJV)

Theme   The Parable of the Wheat and Tares
Type   Exposition/Gospel/Parable
Main Divisions:

   I.   The Items of the Parable
         1. The actors

1) The owner who sows good seed
2) The enemy who sows tares
3) The servants
2. The articles
1) Good seed
2) Tares
3) Field
4) Harvest
5) Barn
6) Fire
3. The action
1) The action of the owner
(1) He sowed bona fide wheat seed in his field
(2) He instructed his servants to wait until the plants were mature
2) The action of the enemy – he sowed tares among the wheat
3) The action of the servants
(1) They waited 'til the harvest time to separate the two lest they damage the good plants
(2) They gathered the good crop in the barn but burned the tares
II. The Interpretation of the Parable
1. The interpretation of the actors
1) The owner is the Lord Jesus Christ who sows the good seed
2) The enemy who sows the tares is the devil
3) The servants (or reapers) are the angels at the end of the age

2. The interpretation of the articles
    1) The good seed is the sons of the Kingdom
    2) The tares are sons of the wicked one
    3) The field is the world
    4) The harvest is the judgment at the end of the age
    5) The barn is heaven
    6) The fire is hell fire
3. The interpretation of the action
    1) The interpretation of the owner's actions
        (1) The Lord Jesus Christ raises up His children in this world
        (2) He has instructed His angels to wait until the end of the age before separating true believers from false brethren
    2) The interpretation of the enemy's action: He raises up his children to mimic the true children of God in order to wreak havoc and destroy God's plan of redemption
    3) The interpretation of the reaper's actions
        (1) The angels presently wait and watch 'til the order is given for them to begin sifting out the children of the devil from true believers
        (2) When they are given the command at the end of the age they will first gather up all the unbelievers of the

world and cast them to hell. Then they will gather up the elect and bring them to heaven

III. The Implications of the Parable
1. Concerning the Lord Jesus
   1) He is actively seeking and saving the lost
   2) He knows the devil's tactics and knows who the false brethren are
   3) He will deal with the problem at the appropriate time
2. Concerning the devil: He is actively working in this world to do nothing other than to thwart the plan of God. He does this by infiltrating true believers with imposters
3. Concerning the false brethren
   1) These false brethren are a different class of unbelievers. They are purposely placed by the devil among true believers in order to wreak havoc
   2) They are so similar to true believers that care must be taken; otherwise one might condemn the innocent along with the guilty. Ultimately, it is their works that will show whether or not they are real. Only when the fruit of their labors becomes evident is it possible to distinguish them from the real thing
   3) They will not escape judgment. Believers must be patient and allow God to sift them from genuine Christians at the proper time

This manner of organizing parabolic passages comes from the master homiletician himself, Dr. John Benson. The idea with this alternate approach is that the expositor examines the parable as a whole rather than its individual parts. We used a very similar approach when we outlined passages with literary analysis. It is exposition, nevertheless, because we are dealing with one passage of Scripture containing more than a few verses. We are using a different technique, however, in the creation of the main divisions.

Typically we create main points as we progress in a "linear" fashion through the verses and notice when a change of subject matter occurs. Here, on the other hand, we are describing the contents of the parable by virtue of identifying the major facets that make up and explain the passage in its entirety. For example, we notice the *items*, the *interpretation*, and the *implications* of this parable. This example is a good format to follow when outlining the parables. If a parable yields other significant points your divisions must reflect them. For example, if the parable contains prophesy then it will probably possess a predictive element and must be stated as a main division. If the parable contains a warning then this also would comprise a major division.

THE EPISTLE GENRE

All of the epistles fall into this category whether they are the Pauline or General epistles. As with the other genres the epistles contain a variety of subgenres. Many of them possess large portions of doctrine such as Romans, Galatians, Ephesians, Colossians, and Hebrews. The epistles are direct addresses to their recipients and therefore contain portions of exhortation to repentance, perseverance, and ethical living along with an abundance of personal appeals. The books of Jude and 2 Peter, on the other hand, are largely invective. Smaller portions of hymns, doxological ideas, and quotes from both biblical and non-biblical sources can be found scattered here and there. First and Second Thessalonians have large sections of prophecy while the doctrinal passages occasionally contain mystical texts as well. Depending upon the writer the style differs greatly. Paul is very personal in his letters to the Corinthians, Galatians, and 1 and 2 Timothy. He uses many references to sports and his knowledge of the Old Testament is obvious. James' writing style, on the other hand, is replete with rich metaphors, something lacking in Paul's letters. Peter's sentences are a mile long and John's Greek is choppy and poor. All of these facts make creating sermons both interesting and challenging.

Doctrinal

Example: Rom. 5:12-21

12 Therefore, just as through one man sin entered the world, and death through sin, and thus death spread to all men, because all sinned— 13 (For until the law sin was in the world, but sin is not imputed when there is no law. 14 Nevertheless death reigned from Adam to Moses, even over those who had not sinned according to the likeness of the transgression of Adam, who is a type of Him who was to come. 15 But the free gift is not like the offense. For if by the one man's offense many died, much more the grace of God and the gift by the grace of the one Man, Jesus Christ, abounded to many. 16 And the gift is not like that which came through the one who sinned. For the judgment which came from one offense resulted in condemnation, but the free gift which came from many offenses resulted in justification. 17 For if by the one man's offense death reigned through the one, much more those who receive abundance of grace and of the gift of righteousness will reign in life through the One, Jesus Christ.)

18 Therefore, as through one man's offense judgment came to all men, resulting in condemnation, even so through one Man's righteous act the free gift came to all men, resulting in justification of life. 19 For as by one man's disobedience many were made sinners, so also by one Man's obedience many will be made righteous. 20 Moreover the law entered that the offense might abound. But where sin abounded, grace abounded much more, 21 so that as sin reigned in death, even so grace might reign through righteousness to eternal life through Jesus Christ our Lord. (NKJV)

Theme   The Contrast Between Condemnation and Salvation
Type   Exposition/Doctrinal
Main Divisions:

I.   The Plague (12-14)
    1. It is infectious (12a, b, c)
    2. It is iniquitous (12d)
    3. It is inevitable (13-14)
II.   The Parallel (15-19)
    1. The Comparison (15-17)
        1) Offense vs. the free gift (15)
        2) Judgment vs. justification (16)
        3) Adam vs. Christ (17)
    2. The Conclusion (18-19)
        1) One man's offense - judgment on all
             One man's righteousness- salv. to all
        2) One man's disobedience- many sinners
             One man's obedience- many righteous
III.   The Prospect (20-21)
    1. Grace defeats guilt (20)
    2. Eternal life defeats death (21)

Example: Rom. 6:1-23

Please refer to this passage and return here in order to examine this outline for yourself.

Theme   The Believer's Death to Sin
Type   Exposition/Epistle/Doctrinal
Main Divisions:

I.   The Believer's Death to Sin Positionally (1-14)
    1. Question: *If grace is a gift to sinners, must we continue to sin to get it?* (1)
    2. Answer: *We cannot sin because we are dead to it* (2)
       1) The crux of our death to sin: *The union of spiritual baptism* (3-5)
         (1) Into His death (3-4a)
         (2) Into His life (4b-5)
       2) The corollary of our death to sin: *Body of sin destroyed* (6-7)
         (1) The means of this destruction of sin: *crucifixion* (6)
         (2) The merits of this destruction of sin: *dead people can't sin* (7)
       3) The conclusion of our death to sin: *Resurrection life* (8-10)
         (1) Resurrection life stated (8)
         (2) Resurrection life sustained (9-10)
       4) The counsel b/c of our death to sin (11-14)
         (1) The particulars (11-13)
            1. Reckon *i.e. bank on it that we are dead to sin and alive to God* (11)

  2. Renounce *i.e. actual sin in our lives* (12)

  3. React *i.e. to the truth of who we are in Christ and live it* (13)

 (2) The promise (14)

II. The Believer's Death to Sin Practically (15-23)

 1. Question: *Since grace came apart from the restraining influence of the Law, does that mean we are free to sin?* (15)

 2. Answer: *By no means! Whatever we yield to we become its slave* (16)

  1) The believer's past slavery to sin (17-18)

   (1) Disobedience to lies made us slaves to sin (17a)

   (2) Obedience to the truth made us slaves to righteousness (17b-18)

  2) The believer's present slavery to righteousness (19-23)

   (1) The exhortation to righteous slavery (19-21)

    1. Exhorted through familiar analogies *i.e. the common practice of slavery* (19a)

    2. Exhorted through familiar addictions *i.e. as we gave ourselves to sin so now we must give ourselves to righteousness* (19b-20)

    3. Exhorted through familiar afflictions *i.e. shame and death* (21)

   (2) The emergence of righteous slavery (22-23)

    1. The statement of this fact (22)

    2. The summation of this fact (23)

Doxological

Example: Rom. 11:33-36

O the depth of the riches both of the wisdom and knowledge of God! how unsearchable are his judgments, and his ways past finding out! 34 For who hath known the mind of the Lord? or who hath been his counsellor? 35 Or who hath first given to him, and it shall be recompensed unto him again? 36 For of him, and through him, and to him, are all things: to whom be glory for ever. Amen.

Theme   Praise to God for His Greatness
Type   Exposition/Epistle/Doxological
Main Divisions:

- I.   Praise Him for His Attributes (33a)
  1. Praise for His wisdom
  2. Praise for His knowledge
- II.   Praise Him for His Actions (33b)
  1. Praise for His unsearchable judgments
  2. Praise for His unknowable ways
- III.   Praise Him for His Autonomy (34-35)
  1. He is understood by no one
  2. He is instructed by no one
  3. He is indebted to no one
- IV.   Praise Him for His Absolutism (36)
  1. He is the source
  2. He is the means
  3. He is the end

Testimonial

Example: 2 Cor. 12:1-10

It is not expedient for me doubtless to glory. I will come to visions and revelations of the Lord. 2 I knew a man in Christ above fourteen years ago, (whether in the body, I cannot tell; or whether out of the body, I cannot tell: God knoweth;) such an one caught up to the third heaven. 3 And I knew such a man, (whether in the body, or out of the body, I cannot tell: God knoweth;) 4 How that he was caught up into paradise, and heard unspeakable words, which it is not lawful for a man to utter. 5 Of such an one will I glory: yet of myself I will not glory, but in mine infirmities. 6 For though I would desire to glory, I shall not be a fool; for I will say the truth: but now I forbear, lest any man should think of me above that which he seeth me to be, or that he heareth of me. 7 And lest I should be exalted above measure through the abundance of the revelations, there was given to me a thorn in the flesh, the messenger of Satan to buffet me, lest I should be exalted above measure. 8 For this thing I besought the Lord thrice, that it might depart from me. 9 And he said unto me, My grace is sufficient for thee: for my strength is made perfect in weakness. Most gladly therefore will I rather glory in my infirmities, that the power of Christ may rest upon me. 10 Therefore I take pleasure in infirmities, in reproaches, in necessities, in persecutions, in distresses for Christ's sake: for when I am weak, then am I strong.

Theme   Paul's Testimony of His Heavenly Vision
Type   Exposition/Epistolary/Testimonial
Main Divisions:

    I.   A Heavenly Testimony (1-4)
        1. Presence in heaven (2-3)
        2. Paradise in heaven (4a)
        3. Prose in heaven (4b)
    II.   A Haughty Testimony (5-6)
        1. A timid haughtiness (5)
        2. A truthful haughtiness (6)
    III.   A Humiliating Testimony (7-9a)
        1. A humiliating prevention (7a)
        2. A humiliating pain (7b)
        3. A humiliating plea (8)
        4. A humiliating perfection (9a)
        5. A humiliating paradox (9b-10)

Exhortation/Doctrinal

Example: Phil. 2:5-11

5 Let this mind be in you which was also in Christ Jesus, 6 who, being in the form of God, did not consider it robbery to be equal with God, 7 but made Himself of no reputation, taking the form of a bondservant, and coming in the likeness of men. 8 And being found in appearance as a man, He humbled Himself and became obedient to the point of death, even the death of the cross. 9 Therefore God also has highly exalted Him and given Him the name which is above every name, 10 that at the name of Jesus every knee should bow, of those in heaven, and of those on earth, and of those under the earth, 11 and that every tongue should confess that Jesus Christ is Lord, to the glory of God the Father. (NKJV)

Theme   Jesus Christ: Exaltation Through Humiliation

Type   Exposition/Epistle/Exhortation

Main Divisions:

- I.   His Humiliation (6-8)
  - 1. His deity (6)
    - 1) Embodiment of God (6a)
    - 2) Equality with God (6b)
  - 2. His downgrade (7)
    - 1) Downgraded regarding His characteristics [i.e. attributes] (7a)
    - 2) Downgraded regarding His constitution (7b, c)
      - (1) From divinity to hireling (7a)
      - (2) From deity to humanity (7b)
  - 3. His degradation (8)
    - 1) A willful degradation (8ab)
    - 2) A woeful degradation (8c)
- II.   His Exaltation (9-11)
  - 1. An exalted status (9a)
  - 2. An exalted surname (9b-10)
    - 1) Exalted in comparison (9b)
    - 2) Exalted by curtsy (10)
      - (1) Heaven will bow
      - (2) Earth will bow
      - (3) Hell will bow
  - 3. An exalted statement (11)

Hymn

Example: 2 Tim. 2:11-13

11 This is a faithful saying: For if we died with Him, we shall also live with Him. 12 If we endure, we shall also reign with Him. If we deny Him, He also will deny us. 13 If we are faithless, He remains faithful; He cannot deny Himself. (NKJV)

Theme   The Conditions of a True Relationship with
               God
Type   Exposition/Epistle/Hymn
Main Divisions:

   I.   The Condition for Perpetuity [i.e. eternality] (11)
          If we die we will live
   II.   The Condition for Position (12a)
          If we remain we will rule
   III.   The Condition for Praise (12b)
          If we deny we will be denied
   IV.   The Condition for Perseverance (13)
          If we are faithless He remains faithful

CHAPTER EIGHT

Diagrammatical Analysis and Biblical Exposition

To my knowledge besides *Thematic Preaching* diagrammatical analysis is the only system of sermon preparation that gives the expositor a specific, scientific, and concrete method of creating sermonic outlines from the biblical text. It has been used by seminaries for years aiding young preachers with the arduous task of delivering God's Holy Word. In addition its fundamental goal is to remain faithful to the text allowing it to speak for itself. It has contributed greatly to the field of homiletics with the thousands of preachers who use it to proclaim biblically sound messages on a weekly basis.

THE RULES OF DIAGRAMMATICAL ANALYSIS

The principle behind diagrammatical analysis is to diagram the original language's grammatical structure and then to create all major and minor points of the sermon from that diagram. It uses specific rules in order to do so. The following criteria, though not exhaustive, comes from Lee L. Kantenwein's foundational work on the subject, DIAGRAMMATICAL ANALYSIS.[47]

1. The horizontal base line which forms the basis for major points, major sub points and all subsequent points.
2. The vertical lines which divide the subject and predicate, predicate and direct object; and the slanted lines which indicate indirect object, predicate nominative or predicate adjective, subject complement

---

[47] L. Kantenwein, DIAGRAMMATICAL ANALYSIS (Winona Lake, Indiana: BMH Books, 1979), 64-65.

or object complement. These vertical lines and slanted lines indicate <u>outline divisions</u> upon the horizontal line.

3. The <u>modifiers</u> underneath the base sentence unit(s) upon the horizontal line change and enhance the meaning of the basic unit(s) immediately above.

4. <u>Transitional words</u> found between the horizontal lines and connected by broken lines are not to be incorporated in the outline. These words help the preacher to form his transitional sentence or thoughts between points.

5. As nearly as possible the student should watch the <u>parallel structure</u> his diagram gives to him. This is true whether the parallel structure is horizontal or vertical.

6. Structure must <u>always have more than one point</u> at each level, no matter whether it is a major point, sub point or minor point.

7. Always think in terms of units. Proceed from the larger to the smaller. Observe horizontal and vertical units.

8. The major points of the outline <u>must develop</u> the proposition as stated and in parallel form.

9. Detailed structure is suggested for the understanding of the biblical text. It is <u>not recommended</u> that the preacher preach minor structure to any audience. Major structure is sufficient or the preacher will lose his congregation with detail.

EXAMPLES OF DIAGRAMMATICAL ANALYSIS

Now let's take a look at Kantenwein's example of 2 Pet. 1:19-21.

19 We have also a more sure word of prophecy; whereunto ye do well that ye take heed, as unto a light that shineth in a dark place, until the day dawn, and the day star arise in your hearts: 20 Knowing this first, that no prophecy of the scripture is of any private interpretation. 21 For the prophecy came not in old time by the will of man: but holy men of God spake as they were moved by the Holy Ghost.

Proposition: The apostle Peter makes two declarations concerning the place of God's Word in the lives of His people.

I. The declaration concerning the priority of the Word (19a) *"We have also a more sure word of prophecy"*

    1. The possession of the priority item *"We have"*

        1) It is continuous (present tense)

        2) It is personal (1st person plural)

        3) It is ownership (we have)

    2. The description of the priority item *"more sure word of prophecy"*

        1) The essence of that description *"word"*

        2) The amplification of that description *"a more sure word of prophecy"*

            (1) Amplified as to trustworthiness

                a. Involving stability *"sure"*

                b. Involving comparison *i.e. w/ comparative adjective*

            (2) Amplified as to its character *"prophecy"*

            (3) Amplified as to its individuality *"the"*

II. The declaration concerning one's practice in relation to the word (19b-21)

    1. The practice summarized *"ye do"*

        1) Summarized as continuous – *present tense*

        2) Summarized as active- *"do"*

2. The practice spelled out *"ye do well that ye take heed"*
   1) Spelled out as to its quality *"well"*
   2) Spelled out as to its activity *"that ye take heed"*
      (1) The essence of the activity
      (2) The explanation of the activity
         a. Explained as to the content dealt with
         b. Explained by comparison
         c. Explained as to its continuance
            i. Continuance until the second coming
            ii. Continuance until the personal result of the Second Coming
   3) Spelled out as to its attitude (20-21)
      (1) The explanation of the attitude
      (2) The object affected by the attitude[48]

Before going further, let's see how Kantenwein derived these divisions using the above criteria for creating his points. Looking at his first major division I. *The declaration concerning the priority of the word* we can see that he derives this from the first horizontal line in verse 19. It looks as follows:

---

[48] Kantenwein, 80-86.

subject & verb (ekomen- we have)|object (word)

|sure
|prophecy
|the ("a" in KJV)

Kantenwein states that all major and minor points come from the horizontal lines (criterion #1). The main horizontal line above containing the subject and predicate serves the basis for the first major division *The declaration concerning the priority of the word*. When the horizontal line is divided with vertical lines (criterion #2 above) separating subject, predicate, object etc., we are able to derive the subpoints of his first major division. That is, the *possession* of the word and the *description* of the word. The Apostle Paul's statement *"We have"* tells us that the word is in our possession. His subpoints of that division come from parsing the Greek verb 'echomen' we have.

Kantenwein's second subpoint under his first main division, *the description of the word*, comes from the predicate being separated from the subject with a vertical line: A *more sure word of prophecy, etc.* This point describes the word that is in our possession. Interestingly, Kantenwein describes it using something we are very familiar with: The "aspects of" approach. That is, the *essence* of that description and the *amplification* of that description. You can view his outline above and notice what the essence actually is and how he amplifies it in his outline.

Our purpose is not to write another book about diagrammatical analysis but simply to understand it and relate it to *Thematic Preaching*. I abbreviated his outline to less than half its original length because Kantenwein went into extreme detail. His point was to give the reader the gist of how diagrammatical outlining works not necessarily to present a homiletical outline that is ready for preaching. He stated that minor structure should not be preached but is only for the preacher's knowledge. He is quite correct because unless his audience consists of seminary Greek students they would never be able to follow such detail.

Let's analyze his outline using the principles of *Thematic Preaching*. First, before beginning the translating and diagramming process the expositor must find the proper theme for 2 Pet. 1:19-21. Kantenwein states in his proposition (which we will call the theme) that the apostle Paul makes two declarations concerning the place of the Word of God in our lives. His two declarations come from the following clauses in the text from which he derives his two main divisions. They are 1) *We have a more sure word of prophecy* and 2) *ye do well that ye take heed . . .* etc.

Like most doctrinal passages the correct theme is fairly specific and straight forward. Paul does, in fact, inform us of the importance of the Word of God in our lives but Kantenwein, perhaps, overstates his case by calling them "declarations." Personally I would not use that term because it is a little strong. After all, the participle *take heed* is conditional in nature. Furthermore, the subject matter of 2 Pet. 1:19-21 naturally divides into three sections not two. Kantenwein acknowledges this fact when he states the following:

However, a more effective sermonic outline would be to make a third major point beginning with the appositional 'hoti' clause (1:20-21).

This means a rewording of the proposition and possible the other two major points.[49]

Indeed, as Kantenwein admits, the third major point should consist of almost all of verses 20-21. These verses speak of Scripture's interpretation and inspiration. They are not, however, stated in the sense of a declaration but rather as a simply known fact. If one chooses to call them declarations for emphasis' sake then I doubt he is seriously misrepresenting the Word of God. That would be nitpicking. I choose to call the theme *The Reliable Word of God.* I think it offers a little more flexibility when creating the divisions. My outline of 2 Pet. 1:19-21 is as follows:

Theme   The Reliable Word of God
Type   Exposition/Epistle/Doctrinal
Main Divisions:

   I.   The Characteristics of the Reliable Word (19a)
      1. It is prophetic
      2. It is positive *i.e. sure, certain*
  II.   The Command of the Reliable Word (19b-e)
      1. Its mandate (19b)
      2. Its metaphors (19c-e)
          1) a light that shineth in a dark place (19c)
          2) the day dawning (19d)
          3) the day star arising in your hearts (19e)
  III.   The Communication of the Reliable Word (20-21)
      1. Reliably Interpreted (20)
      2. Reliably Inspired (21)

---

[49] Kantenwein, 86.

As you can see the outlines are actually similar although mine is simpler. Keeping things as simple as possible cannot be overstated. We both correctly divided 2 Pet. 1:19-21 into the same three sections (as Kantenwein acknowledges). In addition, our themes are fairly similar. There are other things in Kantenwein's criteria that agree with *Thematic Preaching* entirely. If you look at criteria numbers 5-8 you will notice that they echo the principles of *Thematic Preaching* to a "T."

Criterion #5 speaks of "parallel" structure. This is fundamental to *Thematic Preaching*. That is, for consistency's sake the divisions must be expressed in the same way if they describe the same theme. Criterion #6 states that all points must have more than one subpoint. If you break something apart there must be at least two parts. It is only logical. Criterion #7 deals with looking at the subject matter in the verses as units. In other words you must notice the bigger picture and draw the correlation between the parts. Criterion #8, perhaps, is the most important point both to diagrammatical analysis and *Thematic Preaching:* All major divisions must relate to the theme closely. If they do not then either the theme is wrong or your major divisions are wrong. There are **NO** exceptions to this rule.

Should the similarities between the two schools of homiletics be surprising? Their similarities only make sense by virtue of the fact that they are kissing cousins. *Thematic Preaching* seeks to follow the biblical authors' trains of thought (themes) and create the divisions accordingly. Diagrammatical analysis traces the grammar of the text and then creates the divisions. One uses a literary approach and the other uses a grammatical approach. When you have a literary piece of work you also have its grammatical structure behind it. It makes sense that the major divisions, at least, would be similar. That, of course, depends upon the expositor's ability to correctly ascertain the theme, regardless of which school he comes from.

THE STRENGTHS OF DIAGRAMMATICAL ANALYSIS

Its scientific approach. Diagrammatical analysis is the only other system of homiletics that I am aware of that provides a scientific method of creating sermons from the Bible. Diagrammatical analysis is both a system as well as a science that faithfully follows the biblical text. There is no question whether or not an aspiring preacher will be able to create an expository sermon if he learns diagrammatical analysis. He will, in fact, be equipped with a practical tool that will greatly aid him in sermon preparation.

Furthermore diagrammatical analysis agrees with *Thematic Preaching* in many respects. Kantenwein stresses the importance of parallelism, a key tenet of *Thematic Preaching*. He also emphasizes thinking in terms of units. In other words seeing the correlation between the parts of the text and grouping them accordingly. This is crucial to a thematic preacher's task of noticing changes in subject matter. Most significantly he stresses that all of the divisions must relate to the proposition or theme very closely. His sermonic examples are cases in point. His divisions are completely logical and parallel and describe the proposition exactly. For all practical purposes diagrammatical analysis could be considered a subdivision of *Thematic Preaching* emphasizing grammatical diagramming and exegesis.

The priority of the biblical text. Diagrammatical analysis also emphasizes the priority of the biblical text in sermon preparation. It naturally hinders a preacher with the gift of gab from going off on irrelevant, uninspired tangents. It has neither the place nor the tolerance for that behavior in the pulpit. It genuinely seeks to do the biblical text the most justice by emphasizing what the biblical writers have to say according to the grammar and syntax.

The concentration on grammar and exegesis. Diagrammatical analysis' emphasis on grammar, the original languages, and exegesis are tremendous benefits regarding the authority of the sermon. How often is someone in the pew given exegetical proof for what they are told to believe? How often do sermons give the kind of authority that comes along with biblical exegesis and diagramming? While *Thematic Preaching* does justice to the text as well it is up to the expositor to diagram the original languages in order to draw out relevant, syntactical relationships that bear on the interpretation of a text. The English diagram will not always mimic that of the original and can potentially change the meaning of the text. Diagrammatical analysis makes those relationships between words clear. Because the diagrams in the original may differ from their English counterparts it is probable that the major and minor divisions will differ as well. This is a crucial factor. Exegetical accuracy is, perhaps, diagrammatical analysis' greatest strength.

It forces the expositor to learn the original languages. Diagrammatical analysis forces an expositor to learn the biblical languages well. Yes, this is time consuming but it is also a great asset. Knowledge rightly applied is always beneficial and diagrammatical analysis encourages the development of this asset.

THE WEAKNESSES OF DIAGRAMMATICAL ANALYSIS

Certain genres do not lend themselves to be analyzed diagrammatically. *Thematic Preaching* is more versatile and is not restricted by genres of Scripture that do not lend themselves to be analyzed by virtue of a grammatical diagram. I would be very interested in seeing someone create a sermonic outline from passages like Psalm 47 or Job 3 using diagrammatical analysis. I don't mean just a few verses from them but the entire passage. These psalmic texts contain Hebrew parallelism, repetition, and other literary features that do not lend themselves to be analyzed and divided by virtue of a grammatical diagram.

The strength of diagrammatical analysis is also its weakness: Its extreme concentration on grammar blinds itself to the bigger picture that some genres require. It is most effective in the epistolary genre where the sentence structure is straight forward and the themes are easily recognizable. This is not to say that it cannot be used in other genres but the other genres contain literary features that will appear very confusing when put into a grammatical diagram. Can these other genres be diagrammed? Of course, but their diagrams will not be straight forward. There will be such repetition and literary anomalies that the expositor will scratch his head and wonder where he is going. That is because tracing the grammar focuses on the natural, linear flow of the text while blinding the eyes to the big picture. What happens when it is not possible to ascertain the main divisions from a linear standpoint? The grammarian is stumped.

The potential of concentrating on grammar to an extreme. Some important questions are "does grammar and syntax tell us the priority of what is stated or does it simply tell us the relationship between what is stated"? "Does it do both"? "Should main clauses be considered more important than subordinate clauses"? "If they are should they, therefore, serve as the main points and the others as subpoints (circumstances permitting)"? These are questions that linguists and grammarians must answer but my initial thought is that just because something is subordinate grammatically does not mean that it is subordinate practically or literarily.

Consider, for example, the statement "I scribbled in the sand that Jesus died for my sins." Which clause is more important? Is it the main clause "I scribbled in the sand," or is it the subordinate clause "that Jesus died for my sins"? I think the reader knows the answer to that question. Proponents would argue that the issue is not one of importance but of relevance. I don't deny this fact and I am not suggesting that diagrammatical analysis promotes the skewing of grammar in such a manner. I am suggesting, however, that there is a temptation to stress grammar beyond its natural scope and to use a subordinate clause as a subpoint rather than the main point based solely on the fact that it is subordinate grammatically. Invariably there are going to be those who err by making a major point out of something due to the grammar when the natural reading of the text does not warrant it. I spent ten years in theological institutions and, yes, it was something I noticed to be problematic.

Its potential of weighting the expositor down with minutiae. While Kantenwein warns his readers about being bogged down with details the nature of diagrammatical analysis could lead someone down this road very easily. The divisions must be stated as clearly and simply as possible. This is a rule of thumb that I gave early in this book. Awkward and lengthy statements ought to be avoided at all costs. An expositor will lose his audience if his language is not clear and simple. Furthermore he will probably confuse himself, too.

Kantenwein develops a sermonic outline from Psalm 119:17-18. His outline consists of two major divisions with their corresponding subpoints. His second major division is *The Request for Enablement to Understand the Word* (18). One his two subpoints of this division is as follows: *The Outcome of the Request for Enablement to Understand the Word.*[50] While his accuracy is impeccable his language is awkward and he would lose an audience in process of delivering this sermon. I will not throw stones at him because the same tendency is found in my school of homiletics as well. We often sacrifice simplicity for precision. You must have both. You must be able to state the preciseness of your division as simply as possible. As I stated before Dr. Kantenwein's point, no doubt, was not so much to make an outline ready for preaching but to demonstrate the precision of diagrammatical analysis.

Its dependence on the original languages hinders those who don't know them. An obvious concern for those expositors that have not had the privilege of going to a school where Greek and Hebrew are offered is that

---

[50] Kantenwein, Pg. 76.

diagrammatical analysis concerns itself with the original biblical languages, not English. Again, its strength is also its weakness. What can you do if you have never gone to a school that offers these subjects and, therefore, do not have sufficient knowledge to use diagrammatical analysis? Should preaching be limited to those who are thus educated? What about the thousands of pastors around the world in countries where they are very fortunate to have the Bible in their own language not to mention extensive training in Greek and Hebrew? If you diagram the English text of an Old Testament passage you might find out that your English diagram does not do justice to the original Hebrew. Honestly, analyzing things from a literary standpoint is something that can be done in any language, is less time consuming, and much more versatile. We can't be experts in everything.

It is only practical to use for a few verses. Because diagrammatical analysis yields great detail it is really only feasible to use a few verses at a time. Diagrammatical analysis if fine for some passages but what about texts which require more than just a few verses in order to get to the heart and soul of the message? Perhaps there are those who use diagrammatical analysis and can create outlines of entire passages but the rigid concentration of the grammatical diagram naturally limits the outline to a few verses. It is not practical to outline an entire chapter or for that matter an entire book. In Kantenwein's two sermonic examples he uses two verses in his first and three verses in his second. The amount of information diagrammatical analysis yields for those few verses is impressive but it is not conducive for larger portions of Scripture.

Translating and diagramming the original languages is very time consuming. As I was reviewing Kantenwein's book and his sermonic examples I could not help but think how long it would take the average grad from seminary to accomplish the same task. That is another practical reason why using only a few verses is feasible. The better someone is in the biblical languages the faster he will be able to diagram those verses. Even an expert will spend considerable time analyzing everything. Most seminarians and Bible college grads have only an elementary understanding of Greek and far less an understanding of Hebrew. This is not to say that they wouldn't eventually improve but the time required to diagram the original languages and to make sure those diagrams are correct could be prohibitive. You could use someone else's diagrams but then you would not reap the benefits associated with the struggle of learning the language. One thing is for sure, if a pastor only used diagrammatical analysis and faithfully translated the original languages he would be an expert in both Greek and Hebrew by the time he retired. How many of them are, however?

While I have compared the two schools of thought, I hope I have also stressed the fact that the similarities between the two make them related. Why couldn't a thematic preacher use grammatical diagramming in the process? How could it hurt him? It would force him to pay attention to the grammar which is often neglected. The point is, however, that loyalty to one's school prohibits the freedom to be inclusive. The fact is that their similarities reveal that their relationship is not coincidental. Any piece of literature, no matter the genre, has a grammatical structure behind it. When the preacher has the time and ability to analyze both then he truly has complete knowledge of his text.[51]

---

[51] Dr. William D. Ramey, Greek enthusiast, is unique in that his diagrams also portray the discourse analysis as well. This is a very positive step toward a complete system of scriptural analysis. Dr. William Ramey, Inthebeginning.org. http://www.inthebeginning.org (accessed October, 2012).

CHAPTER NINE

The Introduction and Conclusion of the Sermon

My intention for writing this book is not to be an exhaustive treatise on all aspects of preparing and delivering sermons. Its theme is fairly narrow (any wonder?). Most books on homiletics deal with every aspect of preaching from creating the major points to gesticulation to etiquette in the pulpit to the use of humor, etc. If I attempted to accomplish all these tasks it would detract from my main concern of learning the skill of outlining biblical messages. I would be remiss, however, to completely ignore the other parts of the sermon. I have given you the tools in order to create the sermon body but without the introduction and conclusion the body is incomplete.

THE INTRODUCTION

A sermon body might be coherent, possess purpose, and greatly minister to the congregation but without a good introduction it will not be as effective. The introduction safely transitions the preacher's thoughts from his initial remarks into the heart of his message. That is its purpose. Preparing a good introduction is a particularly important skill for young pastors. When I first began preaching on a weekly basis the most difficult task I had was to make the transition into the main body of the sermon. Because my mind was overflowing with information and because of the usual pressure associated with preaching it was the biggest obstacle I had to overcome. I knew that if I could get to the heart of my message I would make it but the journey was not easy.

One way I overcame this was to review in my mind, time and again, my transitional statements. Once a preacher has embedded the sequence of thoughts in his mind beginning with the first word until he reaches the heart of the message he is safe. There is a danger if he cannot accomplish this. It is quite possible for him to lose his place and to become completely disoriented. When that happens it is very hard to pick up the pieces and go on. Preaching requires total concentration. If his mind wanders it could derail him. There are numerous reasons why this might happen - the cry of a baby, a cell phone going off, any other type of distraction, or simply not being prepared sufficiently.

If the preacher is derailed in the heart of his sermon he is much more likely to recover. If, however, this happens during the introduction it could cause the people to go home early. The problem of losing one's place is of greater concern to the novice than to the veteran. An older, seasoned preacher once said that if a pastor has no fear at all when he gets behind the pulpit then something is wrong. This kind of fear is a good thing but it is another factor that a preacher has to deal with and can cause him to lose his place.

Because the purpose of the introduction is to transition to the main body there are several things the preacher can do to assist himself with the task. One of these is to use a vivid illustration or story that paints a picture of what he wants to preach. Illustrations of this nature are very effective and help the preacher keep his own thoughts organized as he transitions to his main sermon body. If a preacher knows specifically the type of illustration he wants to use then it means he also knows what he wants to say. The introduction, therefore, serves as a measuring device as to how prepared he is. Of course there are some who never spend enough time in the study and because they have the gift of gab are quite capable of speaking extemporaneously for as long as it takes. On the other hand, who wants to hear them?

The introduction should not be too lengthy but sufficient to whet the audience's appetite for what follows. There are times when the introduction can be quite long if there is a specific reason for it. I do this on occasion when I feel that a lengthy introduction is necessary in order for the people to know what I am trying to accomplish. If a preacher's total sermon length is 45 minutes then a 5-10 minute introduction would more than sufficient. It could, of course, be shorter as long as the transition to the main body is smooth. As I have gained more experience my introductions have become shorter. I suppose it is because transitioning into the main body of the sermon has become more natural. Like training wheels on a bike once you get the idea you can relax the safeguards. It is never inappropriate, however, to give a good introduction laced with illustrative and interesting information in order to rouse the congregation's curiosity as to what will follow.

THE CONCLUSION

What do you think would happen to an insurance salesman who never asked the customer for a decision? He would not be employed long. The point is that we are preaching to people for a reason. Our sermons must have some purpose behind them. If we are spending countless hours in the study it is because we want the audience to learn something as a result. The purpose of a conclusion is to wrap up the message and encourage its reception. It ties the information together and makes the final applications. The conclusion of the message should be both an emotional and logical appeal to the facts presented. It exhorts the congregation to take the message and apply it to their lives. It is asking them for a decision based upon the biblical mandate contained therein. Many pastors use altar calls, some do not. Regardless, we preach our messages in order for them to be received. Stopping the message at the end of the sermon body is like turning off the movie immediately after the high point. We want to know what the final outcome is but if we don't get the chance to see the ending we will never know. Likewise, the conclusion of the sermon serves to give the message closure.

There are certain techniques that you can use to bring the audience to a decision making point. A good, relevant story is always an excellent device that serves to focus the audience's attention back to the main thrust of the sermon. After sitting for a while it is natural for people's minds to wander. A meaningful story will focus their attention on the spiritual application the preacher is making. A personal testimony or experience by the pastor is also a good way to make the message personal to the congregation. People always appreciate transparency and honesty and when the pastor has firsthand knowledge of a subject it puts the congregation's mind at ease.

Preachers are mandated to speak the truth with love and herein lay the difference between how preachers view their conclusions. Some emphasize the truth more than love and are considered hard while others stress the love aspect and are viewed as being soft. We must learn to strike the proper balance under the guidance of the Holy Spirit and the Word of God. Conclusions that are addressed to a notoriously strong-willed and stubborn congregation must lean on the side of truth. If not then they won't respect the preacher and his message. Jonathan Edward's famous sermon *Sinners in the Hands of an Angry God* was spoken to such an audience. Congregations that have suffered a lot because of death, heart break, etc. need more love.

In either case the preacher's conclusion ought to seek for a response. Even a message geared toward God's unconditional love ought to have a conclusion that causes people to receive that love in some practical way. In all honesty this could be as terrifying for some people as a message on hell. Nevertheless a good conclusion serves to encourage such a decision. The point is, no matter what it takes or what devices the preacher uses the purpose of a conclusion is to tie all the loose ends of the sermon together and to exhort the audience to receive the spiritual lesson.

Lloyd M. Perry and Faris D. Whitesell give some practical pointers regarding the use of conclusions in the sermon:

1. Avoid letting interest lag in the conclusion. Hold sufficient material and force in reserve to make the conclusion that effective climax.
2. Avoid making the conclusion too long. It should be brief and pointed.
3. Avoid giving the impression that you are about to conclude, when you are not.

4. Avoid introducing new material not pertinent to the theme.
5. Avoid concluding a serious message with a joke or humorous remark.
6. Avoid monotony in conclusions. Do not conclude the same way every time. The surprise element and variety in conclusions will help you to achieve your purpose.
7. Avoid trite, hackneyed conclusions. These are indicated by such expressions as, "Now in conclusion, we see," or "Let us apply these truths to our daily lives," or "Let us all try to live closer to the Lord." When a preacher has not properly prepared his conclusion, he will probably fall back on commonplace, general exhortations.
8. Avoid apologizing in the conclusion. If you apologize you will likely call attention to something that many of your hearers have not seen or do not know. When a preacher apologizes, he mistakenly infers that the congregation considers him of more importance than his message.
9. Avoid a formal announcement of your conclusion. If it is been carefully prepared, it will not need in any introductory marks.[52]

---

[52] Lloyd M. Perry and Faris D. Whitesell, <u>Variety in Your Preaching</u> (Flemming H. Revell), 145-146.

CHAPTER TEN

Examples of Expository Outlines

EXAMPLES OF ENTIRE BOOKS OF THE BIBLE

The only subject we have not covered so far in *Thematic Preaching* is how to outline entire books of the Bible. The reader should note that there is a difference between an outline created for the purpose of describing the contents of the book (much like that found in the table of contents) and an outline created for the purpose of preaching. The reason, of course, is that the themes of the passages have a degree of flexibility especially in regard to making spiritual applications. An outline that is intended to be used for a table of contents will appear very straightforward and generic. An outline for a sermon will be altered according to the applications it intends on making.

Dr. John L. Benson gives the following advice concerning making sermonic outlines from an entire book of the Bible.

Try expounding a whole book of the Bible by deciding on a different key word for every chapter in the book and then by developing the chapter around the key-word or key-theme.[53]

Dr. Benson gives an example of such an outline from the book of 1 Thessalonians.

Example: 1st Thessalonians

Theme   The Practical Effects of the Lord's Return
Type   Book Exposition
Main Divisions:

---

[53] Benson, 161.

I. It Produces Examples (Chapter 1)
II. It Promotes Evangelism (Chapter 2)
III. It Provides Establishment (Chapter 3)
IV. It Provokes Exhortation (Chapter 4)
V. It Prompts Expectation (Chapter 5)[54]

This technique works well for books that are relatively short. I personally tried using this approach very early in my preaching career in my church. I decided to preach through the book of Matthew using Benson's advice. What I realized was that using a key word or theme for every chapter of the book did not lend itself well to preaching. The reason is because the information contained in the chapters of the Bible is rarely homogenous.

Archbishop Stephen Langton and Cardinal Hugo de Sancto Caro are credited for including chapters into the books of the Bible in the in the early 13th century. That system is what our modern Bible is based upon. While their work has greatly benefitted us all I think it is safe to say that their work, unfortunately, is not perfect. What does an expositor do when there is a passage that does not relate to the chapter's theme? Gloss over it completely? Stretch and make it fit somehow? Unless the book of the Bible is short and the theme throughout is very consistent I don't think Benson's idea will work well. As you can see, however, for smaller books like 1st Thessalonians it works very well.

I prefer dividing each book of the Bible in the same manner as you would an ordinary passage – by means of subject matter. This requires the expositor to read the

---

[54] Ibid., 164.

book he is preaching through over and over again in order to trace the author's themes. Most books of the Bible are naturally divided into major sections noticeable as the biblical authors shift their trains of thought. These sections should become the largest units of the outline which we will call "parts." Using this approach will yield outlines that favor tables of contents but adaptions can easily be made in order to use them to preach.

When an expositor creates his own outlines without relying on the work of others he can be certain that he will know his material very well. When you use someone else's work it does not become part of you as if you did it yourself. An advantage of *Thematic Preaching's* system of sermon development is that by the time the expositor has perfected his outline he knows the subject matter by heart.

On the other hand it seems a waste not to take advantage of the available outlines created by biblical scholars who spent years developing them. This task is very time consuming. If there is an accurate outline, therefore, that does a good job and follows the rules of *Thematic Preaching* why not refer to it? Why reinvent the wheel? When it comes to fine tuning it for preaching, however, it must have your own adaptation that makes it yours. You can't get away with laziness and use someone else's work entirely.

The following two outlines of the books of Ephesians and Joel are taken from what I consider to be one of the best sources for this purpose: The Open Bible.[55] While The

---

[55] *The Open Bible Expanded Edition,* (Nashville: Thomas Nelson Publishers, 1985).

<u>Open Bible</u> gives no themes with its outlines an expositor can easily deduce them from the contents they contain.

Example: The Book of Ephesians

Part One: The Position of the Christian (1:1-3:21)

I.	Praise for Redemption	1:1-14
	A. Salutation from Paul	1:1-2
	B. Chosen by the Father	1:3-6
	C. Redeemed by the Son	1:7-12
	D. Sealed by the Spirit	1:13-14
II.	Prayer for Revelation	1:15-23
III.	Position of the Christian	2:1-3:13
	A. The Christian's Position Individually	2:1-10
	1. Old Condition: Dead to God	2:1-3
	2. New Condition: Alive to God	2:4-10
	B. The Christian's Position Corporately	2:11-3:13
	1. Reconciliation of Jews/ Gentiles	2:11-22
	2. Revelation: Mystery of Church	3:1-13
IV.	Prayer for Realization	3:14-21

Part Two: The Practice of the Christian (4:1-6:24)

I.	Unity in the Church	4:1-16
	A. Exhortation to Unity	4:1-3
	B. Explanation of Unity	4:4-6
	C. Means for Unity: The Gifts	4:7-11
	D. Purpose of the Gifts	4:12-16
II.	Holiness in Life	4:17-5:21
	A. Put Off the Old Man	4:17-22
	B. Put On the New Man	4:23-29
	C. Grieve Not the Holy Spirit	4:30-5:12
	D. Walk as Children of Light	5:13-17

	E. Be Filled With the Spirit	5:18-21
III.	Responsibilities in the Home/Work	5:22-6:9
	A. Wives: Submit to Your Husbands	5:22-24
	B. Husbands: Love Your Wives	5:25-33
	C. Children: Obey Your Parents	6:1-4
	D. Employees: Submit to your Employers	
		6:5-9
IV.	Conduct in the Conflict	6:10-24
	A. Put on the Armor of God	6:10-17
	B. Pray for Boldness	6:18-20
	C. Conclusion	6:21-24[56]

Example: The Book of Joel

I.	The Day of the Lord in Retrospect	1:1-20
	A. The Past Day of the Locust	1:1-12
	B. The Past Day of the Drought	1:13-20
II.	The Day of the Lord in Prospect	2:1-3:21
	A. The Imminent Day of the Lord	2:1-27
	1. Prophecy of Invasion of Judah	2:1-11
	2. Conditional Promises of the	
	Salv. of Judah	2:12-27
	B. The Ultimate Day of the Lord	2:28-3:21
	1. Last Events Before Terrible Day	2:28-32
	2. Events of the Terrible Day	3:1-21
	a. Judgment of the Gentiles	3:1-15
	b. Restoration of Judah	3:16-21[57]

The themes for these two outlines are easy to detect in spite of the fact that they are not given with the outlines. The introductory notes of each book explain the purpose

---

[56] *The Open Bible*, 1161.
[57] Ibid., 850.

for why the books were written and the themes can be deduced accordingly but, unfortunately, they are not presented with the outlines themselves. Based upon the contents, however, a good theme for the book of Ephesians is *The Christian's Relationship with the Lord*. The key words for the two major parts are *Position* and *Practice*. These denote a relationship. In addition, the major divisions of each part reflect the themes very clearly. You will notice, however, that the major divisions of part one is not completely parallel. The theme for Joel, easily deciphered in the main divisions, is *The Day of the Lord*. The very words in the outline itself indicate that theme. The major divisions in the outline to Ephesians, on the other hand, are conceptually related while in Joel both the words and the concepts reveal the theme.

Another good source for outlines is the The MacArthur Study Bible.[58] The following examples are taken from his study Bible.

Example: The Book of Galatians

    I.   Personal: The Preacher of Justification (1:1-2:21)
          1. Apostolic Chastening (1:1-9)
          2. Apostolic Credentials (1:10-2:10)
          3. Apostolic Confidence (2:11-21)
    II.   Doctrinal: The Principles of Justification (3:1-4:31)
          1. The Experience of the Galatians (3:1-5)
          2. The Blessing of Abraham (3:6-9)
          3. The Curse of the Law (3:10-14)

---

[58] John F. MacArthur Jr., The MacArthur Study Bible (Nashville: Thomas Nelson Pub., 1997).

4. The Promise of the Covenant (3:15-18)
5. The Purpose of the Law (3:19-29)
6. The Sonship of Believers (4:1-7)
7. The Futility of Ritualism (4:8-20)
8. The Illustration from Scripture (4:21-31)
III. Practical: The Privileges of Justification (5:1-6:18)
1. Freedom from Ritual (5:1-6)
2. Freedom from Legalists (5:7-12)
3. Freedom in the Spirit (5:13-26)
4. Freedom from Spiritual Bondage (6:1-10)
5. Conclusion (6:11-18)[59]

Example: The Book of Jonah

I. Running from God's Will (1:1-17)
1. The Commission of Jonah (1:1-2)
2. The Flight of Jonah (1:3)
3. The Pursuit of Jonah (1:4-16)
4. The Preservation of Jonah (1:17)
II. Submitting to God's Will (2:1-10)
1. The Helplessness of Jonah (2:1-3)
2. The Prayer of Jonah (2:4-7)
3. The Repentance of Jonah (2:8,9)
4. The Deliverance of Jonah (2:10)
III. Fulfilling God's Will (3:1-10)
1. The Commission Renewed (3:1,2)
2. The Prophet Obeys (3:3,4)
3. The City Repents (3:5-9)
4. The Lord Relents (3:10)
IV. Questioning God's Will (4:1-11)

---

[59] MacArthur, 2539. The NIV Study Bible is also another good source of outlines.

1. The Prophet Displeased (4:1-5)
2. The Prophet Rebuked (4:6-11)[60]

EXAMPLES OF ACTUAL SERMONS FROM GREAT PREACHERS

I stated in the first chapter that the subject of homiletics cannot be compared to English Grammar. Everyone agrees what the rules of grammar are but, unfortunately, homiletics is not that fortunate. There is no one standard. Each goes at the task from their own set of rules. It is interesting to note, however, that great preachers have certain things in common. The spiritual dynamic is a given but there are other ways in which they are similar. You will notice in the following sermonic outlines that parallelism is something they all demonstrate. The sermons of these preachers are well organized and logically presented – key tenets of *Thematic Preaching*. Above all notice the theme in each of these sermons and how the main points reflect them clearly.

The following outlines are taken from great preachers both of yesterday and today. As you will see they preached thematically long before this book was written. Some of the outlines are written exactly as they were preached while others I have alliterated in order to make the language parallel (even though their thoughts were perfectly parallel). If the following outlines were alliterated by me I have noted that in the footnotes, otherwise they are written exactly as they were preached. As a side note, should the reader visit the web addresses given below in order to listen to the messages they may not find the

---

[60] Ibid., 1879.

sermons as documented. The reason is because the websites have the tendency to update the information and move the information around.

Example: **Dr. Charles F. Stanley**
               Neh. 8:1-7, 12-17, 9:1-3

Theme   You Must Listen to God's Word
Type   Exposition/Historical Narrative
Main Divisions:

I.   Eagerly (8:1-2)
II.   Attentively (8:3)
III.   Trustingly (8:4-5)
IV.   Expectantly (8:5)
V.   Prayerfully (8:6)
VI.   Patiently (8:7)
VII.   Humbly (8:6)
VIII. Purposefully (8:12-17)
IX.   Happily
X.   Repentantly (9:1-3)[61]

Example: **Dr. David Jeremiah**
               James 1:1-12

Theme   What to Do When the Heat's Turned Up
Type   Exposition/Epistle
Main Divisions:

I.   Celebrate the Reason Behind Your Trials (1:2)
II.   Calculate the Results of Your Trials (3-4)
       1. Trials Produce Durability

---

[61] Dr. Charles Stanley, In Touch Ministries. http://www.intouch.org/broadcast/today-on-radio (accessed November, 2012).

       2. Trials Produce Maturity

III.   Call Upon God's Resources in Your Trials (5)
       1. God is Good
       2. God is Generous
       3. God is Gracious

IV.   Consider Your Reactions to Your Trials (9-10)

V.   Contemplate the Rewards of Your Trials (12)[62]

Example: **Dr. David Jeremiah**
              Eph. 6:18

Theme   Praying Always With All Prayer
Type   Textual
Main Divisions:

I.   The Persistence of the Warrior's Prayer

II.   The Possibilities of the Warrior's Prayer
       1. We are to Pray on All Occasions
       2. We are to Pray in All Places
       3. We are to Pray in Prosperity and Adversity
       4. We are to Pray for All Things

III.   The Petition of the Warrior's Prayer

IV.   The Power of the Warrior's Prayer

V.   The Precision of the Warrior's Prayer

VI.   The Perseverance of the Warrior's Prayer[63]

---

[62] Dr. David Jeremiah, Turning Point Ministries. http://www.davidjeremiah.org/site/uploadedfiles/070112%20What%20to%20Do%20When%20the%20Heats%20Turned%20Up.pdf (accessed November, 2012).

[63] Dr. David Jeremiah, Turning Point Ministries. http://www.davidjeremiah.org/site/uploadedfiles/061012%20Praying%20Always%20With%20All%20Prayer.pdf (accessed November, 2012).

Example: Dr. Adrian Rogers
 2 Cor. 5:9-20

Theme   The Soul Winner's Six Mighty Motivations
Type   Exposition/Epistle
Main Divisions:

I.   His Compulsion (9)
II.   His Compensation (10)
III.   His Conviction (11)
IV.   His Compassion (13-15)
V.   His Confidence (16-17)
VI.   His Commission (18-20)[64]

Example: Dr. Adrian Rogers
 Dan. 9:3-21

Theme   How to Pray for America
Type   Exposition/Apocalyptic/Historical Narrative
Main Divisions:

I.   We are to Pray With Serious Concentration (3)
          1. Prayer and Fasting
          2. Proper Motivation for Fasting
          3. To Be Done as unto the Lord
          4. Fasting Strengthens Our Prayer Life
          5. Fasting Holds Back Judgment
          6. How Should We Fast?
II.   We are to Pray With Steadfast Confidence (4,9)
III.   We are to Pray With Serious Confession (4-7)
          1. Daniel Confessed Personal Sin
          2. Daniel Confessed National Sin

---

[64]Dr. Adrian Rogers, Love Worth Finding Ministries.
http://www.lwf.org/site/Search?query=The+Soul+Winner%27s+Six+M
ight+Motivations (accessed November, 2012).

IV. We are to Pray With Spiritual Concern
    1. Daniel was Concerned With the Removal of Guilt (16)
    2. Daniel was Concerned With the Restoration of Glory (17,19)[65]

Example: **John F. MacArthur Jr.**
                      Zech. 12:1-13:9

Theme   The Salvation of Israel
Type   Exposition/Prophesy
Main Divisions:

I.   The Siege of Israel (12:1-6)
II.   The Shielding of Israel (7-9)
III.   The Sorrow of Israel (10-14)
IV.   The Salvation of Israel (13:1-9)[66]

Example: **Charles R. Swindoll**
                      1 Sam. 15:24-16:13

Theme   David: A Man of Passion & Destiny:
                 A Nobody that Nobody Noticed
Type   Exposition/Historical Narrative
Main Divisions:

I.   Man Panics ....God Provides (15:24-16:3)
II.   Man Chooses ....God Corrects (16:4-10)
III.   Man Forgets ....God Remembers (16:11-13)[67]

---

[65] Dr. Adrian Rogers, Love Worth Finding Ministries. http://www.oneplace.com/ministries/love-worth-finding/player/how-to-pray-for-america-288382.html (accessed November, 2012).

[66] Dr. John F. MacArthur Jr., Grace to You Ministries. http://www.gty.org/resources/sermons/90-445/the-salvation-of-israel (accessed November, 2012).

Example: **Charles R. Swindoll**
                     Philemon

Theme   Building a Life that Pleases God:
                    Reinstatement of a Runaway
Type   Exposition/Epistle
Main Divisions:

    I.   Introduction to Philemon (1-3)
    II.   Commendation to Philemon (4-7)
    III.   Intercession to Philemon (8-17)
    IV.   Obligation of Philemon (18-22)[68]

Example: **Pastor Alan Carr**
                     1 Thess. 4:13-17

Theme   When Jesus Comes!
Type   Exposition/Epistle
Main Divisions:

    I.   There will Be a Resurrection (13-15)
          1. There is a Word About a Situation (13)
          2. There is a Word About a Location (14)
          3. There is a Word About an Affirmation (15)
    II.   There will Be a Rescue (16-17)
          1. It Will be Sudden (17)
          2. It Will be Selective (17)
          3. It Will be Serious

---

[67]Charles Swindoll, Insight for Living Ministries.
http://www.insightforliving.com/pdf/retailseries/David_MessageMate
s.pdf (accessed November, 2012).
    [68]Charles Swindoll, Insight for Living Ministries.
http://www.insightforliving.com/pdf/retailseries/CharacterCounts_M
essageMates.pdf (accessed November, 2012).

4. It Will be Sensational
III. There Will be a Reunion (17)
1. We Will Meet the Saints (17a)
2. We Will Meet the Savior (17b)[69]

Example: **Woodrow Kroll**
Matt. 27:57-28:7

Theme   Three Questions of Easter
Type   Exposition/Gospel
Main Divisions:

I. What Kind of Security Does Satan Have? Matt. 27:57-66
1. The Stone 27:57-61
2. The Seal vv. 62-66
3. The Soldiers vv. 65-66

What kind of security? INADEQUATE

II. What Kind of Servants Does Jesus Have? Matt. 28:1-5
1. The Women 28:1
2. The Earthquake v. 2
3. The Angel vv. 2-5

What kind of servants? OBEDIENT

III. What Kind of Savior Do We Have? Matt. 28:6-7
1. A Savior Who KEEPS HIS WORD v. 6
2. A Savior Who CONQUERS DEATH v. 6
3. A Savior WORTH TALKING ABOUT v. 7[70]

---

[69] Pastor Alan Carr, Sermonnotebook.org. http://www.sermonnotebook.org/new%20testament/1%20Thessalonians%204_13-18.html (accessed November, 2012).

Example: **Dr. Woodrow Kroll**
Luke 2:8-20

Theme   Everyone Loves a Baby
Type   Exposition/Gospel
Main Divisions:

    I.   Baby Jesus Changed the Shepherds' Position (9-11)

    II.   Baby Jesus Changed the Shepherds' Priorities (15-16)

    III.   Baby Jesus Changed the Shepherds' Purposes (17-18)

    IV.   Baby Jesus Changed the Shepherds' Perspectives (20)[71]

Example: **George Whitefield**
Jer. 6:14

Theme   The Method of Grace: *How Can We Speak Peace to Our Hearts?*
Type   Textual
Main Divisions:

    I.   Negatively
         1. We Must Cry for our Iniquities
         2. We Must Comprehend our Inadequacies
         3. We Must Condemn our Infidelity

---

[70] Dr. Woodrow M. Kroll, e-mail message to the author, December 18th, 2012. Dr. Kroll preached this on his tour through the Holy Land and these outlines.

[71] Dr. Woodrow M. Kroll, e-mail message to the author, December 18th, 2012. Dr. Kroll preached this on his tour through the Holy Land.

II. Positively: We Must Lay Hold on the Imputed Righteousness of Christ[72]

Example: **Charles Finney**
Luke 16:2

Theme   What Stewards Must Give Account For
Type   Topical
Main Division:

    I. Stewards will Account for their Time
    II. Stewards will Account for their Talents
    III. Stewards will Account for their Influence
    IV. Stewards will Account for their Property
    V. Stewards will Account for their Soul
    VI. Stewards will Account for their Thoughts
    VII. Stewards will Account for their Opportunities[73]

Example: **Charles H. Spurgeon**
Gal. 6:14

Theme   The Cross Our Glory
Type   Textual
Main Divisions:

    I. What is the Essence of the Cross?
        1. The Phenomenon of the Cross
        2. The Precepts of the Cross
        3. The Person of the Cross
    II. Why Exult in the Cross?
        1. It Defends Divine Law
        2. It Displays Divine Love

---

[72] Jerry Falwell, <u>25 of the Greatest Sermons Ever Preached</u> (Lynchburg: Old Time Gospel Hour Pub., 1983), 18-24. The words of this outline have been adapted but match Whitefield's points exactly.
[73] Ibid., 66-72.

       3. It Dispenses Divine Liability

III.   What is the Effect of the Cross?

       1. A Disdain for the World's Approval

       2. A Disgust for the World's Acumen

       3. A Disinterest with the World's Achievements[74]

Example: **D. L. Moody**

               Matt. 22:42

Theme   What Think Ye of Christ?

Type   Topical

Main Divisions:

I.   What Do You Think of Him?

       1. As a Teacher?

       2. As a Healer?

       3. As a Comforter?

II.   What Do the Witnesses Think of Him?

       1. The Witness of the Pharisees

       2. The Witness of Caiaphas

       3. The Witness of Pilate

       4. The Witness of Judas

       5. The Witness of the Centurion

       6. The Witness of the Repentant Thief

       7. The Witness of His Friends

       8. The Witness of Peter

       9. The Witness of John

       10. The Witness of Paul

       11. The Witness of the Other World

          1) The Lost

          2) The Redeemed

---

[74] Ibid., 76-86. The words of outline are adapted but reflect the sermon content exactly.

12. The Witness of the Father[75]

Example: **T. DeWitt Talmage**
             Rev. 1:8

Theme   Christ: The A and the Z
Type   Topical
Main Divisions:

    I.   He is the A and the Z of the Physical Universe
    II.   He is the A and the Z of the Bible
    III.   He is the A and the Z of Christian Ministry
    IV.   He is the A and the Z in the World's Rescue
    V.   He is the A and the Z in Heaven[76]

Example: **J. Wilbur Chapman**
             2 Kings 20:15

Theme   An Old Fashioned Home
Type   Topical
Main Divisions:

    I.   The Two Great Principles of the Home
        1. Authority
        2. Example
    II.   The Two Great Forces in the Home
        1. Father
        2. Mother[77]

---

[75] Ibid., 90-96.
[76] Ibid., 108-113.
[77] Ibid., 152-159.

Example: **George W. Truett**
                  Rev. 1:17-18

Theme   The Conquest of Fear
Type   Textual
Main Divisions:

    I.   Jesus Bids Us to be Unafraid of Life
    II.   Jesus Bids Us to be Unafraid of Death
    III.   Jesus Bids Us to be Unafraid of Eternity[78]

Example: **G. Campbell Morgan**
                  John 8:28-30

Theme   Christ: The Perfect Ideal of Life
Type   Exposition/Gospel
Main Divisions:

    I.   His Spirituality
    II.   His Subjection
    III.   His Sympathy
    IV.   His Strength[79]

---

[78] Ibid., 196-202.
[79] Ibid., 206-211.

Example: **R.G. Lee**
              1 Kings 21

Theme   Pay Day-Some Day
Type   Exposition/Historical Narrative
Main Divisions:

I.   The Real Estate Request
II.   The Pouting Potentate
III.   The Wicked Wife
IV.   The Message Meaning Murder
V.   The Fatal Fast
VI.   The Visit to the Vineyard
VII.   The Alarming Appearance
VIII.   Pay Day-Some Day[80]

---

[80] Ibid., 234-254. This message by R. G. Lee is parallel in spite of the fact that it may not be immediately recognizable. Each main division is characterized as a title rather than an aspect of the theme. Each alliterative main division depicts another aspect of the coming judgment on wicked Ahab and Jezebel.

CHAPTER ELEVEN

Spiritual Matters

While this is the last chapter of the book it is also, undeniably, the most important. When I began writing *Thematic Preaching,* I wanted to keep my task straight forward and simple. I wanted to expound upon the most logical and versatile system of homiletics ever devised. I did not want to talk about the other aspects of sermon preparation that warrant attention at the proper time and place. I simply wanted to focus on developing sermonic outlines. There are countless other good books on the subject that exhaustively cover every aspect of sermon preparation. By the same token I could not ignore the most important aspect of preaching: The Holy Spirit's empowerment. I stated in the first chapter that the spiritual element was more significant than anything else. If someone masters *Thematic Preaching* but ignores the spiritual dynamic he has accomplished absolutely nothing other to bring attention to himself. Our goal, on the other hand, is to glorify our Lord and Savior Jesus Christ.

The first spiritual element that warrants attention is a pastor's call to preach. When we think of famous preachers who have faithfully delivered God's Word we know intuitively that they have a calling from God and that there is something unique about their Christian walk. Their success lay not in their own abilities but in God's presence with them in a dynamic way. Success does not necessarily mean that their churches are packed or that their ministries are televised. Rather it means that the Spirit has freedom to use these men to proclaim His will. An appropriate name for the Spirit's empowerment is called the anointing. If someone does not have the anointing of God he will not be successful.

The anointing cannot be mimicked. If it is not genuine people will know because of the lack of the movement of the Holy Spirit. The power of the Holy Spirit cannot be forced. The anointing is not necessarily given to a man because he asks for it. God sovereignly gives gifts to his children with the reality that some are called while others are not. If they are not called then preaching as a vocation would neither be fulfilling nor enjoyable. The first thing for a man to recognize is whether or not God has called him. How does someone know? Do they enjoy it? Are they satisfied doing it to the point that they don't want to do anything else? Does the Spirit move when they preach?

I heard the late Dr. Jerry Falwell say that when he was a young, aspiring minister he asked God for a sign to show him whether or not he was called to preach. He got his answer when he delivered his very first message. During the invitation an old woman who was a charter member of that church came down to the altar and gave her life to Christ. Dr. Falwell took that as a sign from God that he was, indeed, called to proclaim the Gospel. He did so until the day he died.

The next spiritual factor worthy of our attention is the submission to the Holy Spirit's leading. A pastor may be called but that does not mean the Spirit automatically anoints every message his preaches. Being called is only the first step to the accomplishment of God's will in the pulpit. The calling means that God has authorized him and will empower him if he learns to submit to His Spirit. If a man is not authorized by God he will never be used mightily. Submitting to the Spirit means that the preacher has learned to get out of the way and to the let Christ speak through him. I recall one Sunday morning as a guest worship leader was introducing me to preach that he petitioned a very interesting request for me. I remember him praying succinctly "Lord, get this man out of the way and preach in his place." That was quite a prayer and I received it in spite of a little squirming in the process. Self needs to be eradicated. *"If any man speak, let him speak as the oracles of God"* (1 Pet. 4:11).

The first area that is necessary to surrender to the Spirit is deciding what to preach. Expository preaching means that the pastor is preaching through a book or passage in a sequential manner so that the subject matter is already laid out for him. This does not mean, however, that the preacher already knows the best way to handle that passage. The same is true for topical and textual messages. A good understanding of the subject matter, a keen intellect, and a natural proclivity for public speaking may be hindrances instead of benefits if the man has not learned to get out of the way and to let the Holy Spirit preach through him. To get out of the way means to become utterly vulnerable and to have nothing to say unless God helps you. This is why there ought to be a little fear each time you step into the pulpit. It demonstrates that you realize that you are in trouble if God does not help you at that moment.

John Hyde was a missionary to India during the turn of the 20th century. He became famous not because he was good at learning new languages – in fact, he had a hearing disability and language learning for him was tough. Nor was he famous because of his ability to eloquently expound God's Word. He became famous because of his extraordinary prayer life. His utter selflessness in prayer led him to a premature death due to his disciplined, rigorous prayer life that took a toll on his health. Upon examination the doctors insisted that he change his lifestyle because his internal organs had moved out of their original places, a consequence of his body being in a posture of prayer for countless hours every day. We remember him by his immortal appellation: *Praying Hyde*.

If you asked Hyde to pray for you you would have gotten more than you bargained for. He would take you aside at that very moment, with or without your consent, and begin his prayer with a deep sigh of acknowledgement. As you stood quiet and motionless five minutes later he would utter "Oh God!" After 40 minutes or so he might finally break through and utter such petitions for you that you knew God would grant those requests. Nothing was trite to him when it came to the Lord his God.

On one occasion he was assigned to preach at a missionary conference. When it came time in the program for him to speak a man made the mistake by coming over to him saying, "Brother John, if you have a message from God, now would be the time to give it." Confused, disturbed, John arose and immediately left the conference hall. Apparently that statement bothered him because he was not 100% sure that his message was, indeed, from God. The person in charge of the conference stated later that there was at least one obedient man in that auditorium. John was not concerned with the etiquette of men but with the honor of God. His life and testimony are a lesson to us all of what priority the Holy Spirit ought to have in our preaching.

How does one know whether or not he has surrendered to the Holy Spirit? I suppose there could be numerous answers to that question but what comes to my mind is the willingness to release control. There is a lot of pressure associated with delivering God's Word. There are pressures from people who are listening to every word intently. There are pressures associated with spiritual warfare. There are also pressures associated with the fear of failure, etc. These pressures make it easy for us to capitulate to our fears and seize control of the situation. When this happens we are not under the power of the Holy Spirit but are operating in our own strength and wisdom. It takes a lot of courage to face our fears and surrender them to Jesus Christ insisting that unless He preaches through us we are going to fail. That place of vulnerability is absolutely uncomfortable but the benefits it yields are incredible. The obvious proof is the power of the sermon itself and the testimony of the people who were blessed by it. Nothing could be more rewarding. If preaching is a gift from God, then we ought to let Him preach us.

All of us who have the responsibility of delivering God's Word know the pressures associated with preaching. There is always struggle. Sometimes messages come easy and sometimes they don't. We ought never to become complacent regardless of how easy the messages come. Struggling during preparation does not necessarily mean that we are operating in our own flesh. Who of us can claim total victory over that? It might mean that God is wrestling with us as He did with Jacob in order to bring about His will in the pulpit. We ought never to get discouraged if the preparation is particularly hard. We have no idea what spiritual forces are at work that are opposed to God's Word being spoken effectively. We ought never to become judgmental either of ourselves or of anyone else who might be experiencing this.

If for some reason I am having a particularly difficult time during preparation I make it a point to go over the message in my head time and time again. This is a good practice regardless of the level of difficulty. While I am doing this I also simultaneously pray diligently that God would help me. It is a good idea to get alone in a quiet room and with vocal cords reverberating preach to the wall until we know that our thought process is on the right track. Anything that does not belong or is causing trouble will, in fact, come to the surface. These mock trials are very valuable for bringing everything together and revealing anything that doesn't belong. They permit God to work in us as we are struggling to preach what He desires. They force us to become vulnerable as we are sincerely trying to glorify Him and not our own genius.

If being called and being submissive to the Spirit are absolutely essential elements of godly preaching then I shouldn't have to say that our personal lives must be in accord with the message we are proclaiming to others. One of the greatest benefits of preaching the Gospel is that we have the opportunity of applying to ourselves the very things we tell others. There is no getting around it. If I am preaching through the book of 1st Corinthians and I come to passages that denounce gossip and excessive anger I have the responsibility to repent and address my own flaws before preaching the same thing to my congregation. This is a tremendous blessing. By the same token I realize that we all have weaknesses and perfect repentance is not a practical reality. I can at least, however, be honest about my shortcomings and acknowledge them before the Almighty. If my congregation has been on the receiving end of my carnal traits then, unfortunately, I have no choice but to acknowledge them before them as well. If I don't I will invariably weaken the authority of God's Word. That would be unacceptable.

The last spiritual element I will mention in this chapter is the expositor's passion for delivering God's Word. This is not only an emotional, mental, or physical element but, in fact, a spiritual element as well. If I am delivering God's Word and I am not enthusiastic about it then why should the congregation be? I am not referring to a particular personality type. God calls every kind of personality to preach His Word. He calls naturally monotone speakers. He calls excitable and loud preachers and He calls everything in between. Being monotone does not necessarily mean that the preacher doesn't care. It is simply the way he is wired and how he expresses himself. Arguably, Jonathon Edwards preached one of the most effective sermons ever in a perfectly monotone voice with his famous sermon *Sinners in the Hands of an Angry God*. People can tell, nevertheless, whether a preacher really cares about what is he saying.

If you are in an emotional rut and can't seem to engender any feelings at all then you need to pray until you feel God is with you regardless of the feeling. God will give breakthrough if we persevere through the difficult times. I would not be too concerned about measuring up to someone else's definition of passion either. Possessing passion for God's Word is only natural. If you do not speak with passion be careful that you are not falling into the trap of apathy. Your audience knows.

Homiletician Lloyd M. Perry pertinently quotes V. L. Stanfield regarding evangelistic preaching. This closing paragraph is a suitable ending to *Thematic Preaching*. May its usefulness assist you to proclaim God's Word effectively, logically, coherently, purposefully, and spiritually:

First, it (i.e. the evangelistic sermon) should be marked by zeal or enthusiasm. When the preacher realizes that the destiny of the human soul is at stake, he cannot speak flippantly. The concern in his heart should show in his delivery. A preacher should speak quietly until his inner feelings demand that he speak enthusiastically. Secondly, ... the evangelistic sermon should be noted for freedom of delivery. Finally, above all other preaching, evangelistic preaching must be completely dependent upon the Holy Spirit.[81]

---

[81] Lloyd M. Perry, <u>Biblical Preaching for Today's World</u> (Chicago: Moody Press, 1973), 160.

BIBLIOGRAPHY

Anderson, F.I. <u>Job: An Introduction and Commentary</u>. Downers Grove, Ill.: InterVarsity Press, 1976.

Benson, John L. <u>A System of Homiletics</u> 3rd ed. Bible School Park, NY: by the author, 1986.

Blackwood, Andrew W. <u>Expository Preaching for Today</u>. New York: Abingdom-Cokesbury Press, 1953.

_____. <u>The Preparation of Sermons</u>. New York: Abingdom-Cokesbury Press, 1948.

Braga, James. <u>How to Prepare Bible Messages</u>. Portland, OR: Multnoma Press, 1981.

Brooks, Phillip. <u>Lectures on Preaching</u>. Grand Rapids: Baker Book House, 1969.

Bullock, Hassell. <u>An Introduction to the Old Testament Poetic Books</u>. Chicago: Moody Press, 1988.

Dolan, David. <u>Holy War for the Promised Land</u>. Nashville: Thomas Nelson Publishers, 1991.

Falwell, Jerry. <u>25 of the Greatest Sermons Ever Preached</u>. Lynchburg: Old Time Gospel Hour Pub., 1983.

Fee, Gordon D. and Douglas Stuart. <u>How to Read the Bible for All Its Worth</u>. Grand Rapids: Zondervan, 1982.

Gaebelein, Frank E. ed. <u>The Expositor's Bible Commentary</u>. Grand Rapids: Zondervan, 1993.

Greidanus, Sidney. <u>The Modern Preacher and the Ancient Text</u>. Grand Rapids: Eerdmans, 1988.

Greidanus, Sidney. <u>Sola Scriptura: Problems and Principles in Preaching Historical Texts</u>. Toronto: Wedge, 1970.

Habel, N.C. *The Book of Job*. <u>The Cambridge Bible Commentary on the N.E.B</u>. Cambridge: Cambridge University Press, 1975.

Kantenwein, Lee. <u>DIAGRAMMATICAL ANALYSIS</u>. Winona Lake, Indiana: BMH Books, 1979.

Kaiser, Walter C., Jr. <u>Ecclesiastes: Total Life</u>. Chicago: Moody Press, 1979.

Killinger, John. <u>The Centrality of Preaching in the Total Task of the Ministry</u>. Waco, TX: Word Books, 1969.

Koller, Charles W. <u>Expository Preaching Without Notes</u>. Grand Rapids: Baker Book House, 1962.

Kroll, Woodrow Michael. <u>The Prescription for Preaching</u>. Grand Rapids: Baker Book House, 1980.

Lenski, T.C.H. <u>The Sermon, Its Homiletical Construction</u>. Columbus: The Luthern Book Concern, 1927.

Long, Thomas G. <u>Preaching and the Literary Forms of the Bible</u>. Philadelphia: Fortress, 1989.

Longman, Tremper, III. <u>How to Read the Psalms</u>. Downer's Grove, Ill.: InterVarsity Press, 1988.

_____. <u>Literary Approaches to Biblical Interpretation</u>. Grand Rapids: Zondervan, 1987.

MacArthur John F. Jr. *The Book of Revelation Vol. 1*. <u>The MacArthur New Testament Commentary</u>. Chicago: Moody Press, 1999.

MacArthur, John F. Jr. The MacArthur Study Bible. Nashville: Thomas Nelson Pub., 1997.

Morgan, G. Campbell. The Ministry of the Word. Grand Rapids: Baker Book House, 1970.

Mounce, Robert. The Essential Nature of New Testament Preaching. Grand Rapids: Eerdmans, 1960.

The Open Bible. Expanded Edition. Nashville: Thomas Nelson Publishers, 1985.

Perrine, Laurence. Literature, Structure, Sound, and Sense. 5th ed. New York: Harcourt Brace Jovanovich Publishers, 1988.

Perry, Lloyd M. Biblical Preaching for Today's World. Chicago: Moody Press, 1973.

Perry, Lloyd M. and Faris D. Whitesell. Variety in Your Preaching. Old Tappan, NJ: Flemming H. Revell Co., 1953.

Robertson, David. *The Bible as Literature.* Supplementary Volume. The Interpreter's Dictionary of the Bible. Keith Crim, ed. Nashville: Abington Press, 1976.

Ryken, Leland. How to Read the Bible as Literature. Grand Rapids: Zondervan, 1984.

_____. The Literature of the Bible. Grand Rapids: Zondervan, 1974.

_____. Words of Delight. Grand Rapids: Baker, 1987.

_____. Words of Life: A Literary Introduction to the New Testament. Grand Rapids: Baker, 1988.

Ryken, Leland and Tremper Longman. eds. A Complete Literary Guide to the Bible. Grand Rapids: Zondervan, 1988.

Shedd, William G.T. Homiletics and Pastoral Theology. New York: Charles Scribner's Sons, 1895.

Silva, Moise's. God, Language, and Scripture. Vol. 4. Foundations of Contemporary Interpretation. ed. Moise's Silva. Grand Rapids: Zondervan, 1990.

Spurgeon, Charles Haddon. Lectures to My Students. Grand Rapids: Zondervan, 1965.

Steckel, Coach Les. One Yard Short. Nashville: Thomas Nelson Publishers, 2006.

Stidger, William L. Building Sermons with Symphonic Themes. New York: George Doran Company, 1926.

_____. Preaching out of the Overflow. Nashville: Cokesbury Press, 1929.

Storrs, Richard S. Preaching Without Notes. Cincinnati: Jennings and Graham, 1875.

Stott, John R.W. The Preacher's Portrait. Grand Rapids: Eerdmans, 1961.

Unger, Merrill, F. Unger's Commentary on the Old Testament. Vol. II. Chicago: Moody Press, 1981.

_____. Principles of Expository Preaching. Grand Rapids: Zondervan, 1955.

Whitesell, Faris D. The Art of Biblical Preaching. Grand Rapids: Zondervan, 1950.

Wood, John. The Preacher's Workshop: Preparation for Expository Preaching. Chicago: InterVarsity Press, 1965.

Worley, Robert C. Preaching and Teaching in the Earliest Church. Philadelphia: The Westminster Press, 1967.